JOURNEY
TOWARDS THE
UNKNOWABLE
The Infinite and the Eternal

POONAM SHARMA

JOURNEY TOWARDS THE UNKNOWABLE:
The Infinite and the Eternal
Author: Poonam Sharma

Referenced material:

[1] **Author Jane Roberts, notes by Robert F Butts** A Seth Book *The Nature of Personal Reality*, Specific, Practical Techniques for solving everyday problems and enriching the life you know *(1974 Co-published by Amber-Allen Publishing and New World Library)*

[2] **Author Eckhart Tolle**, *The Power of Now*, A GUIDE TO SPIRITUAL ENLIGHTENMENT *(1999 New World Library and Namaste Publishing)*

[3] **Author Eckhart Tolle**, *A New Earth,* Awakening to Your Life's Purpose *(2005, 2016 PENGUIN BOOKS)*

Copyright © 2020 by Poonam Sharma
ISBN: 978-1-7321916-4-8
Edited by: Michael Pinchera
Design & Layout by: Douglas DoNascimento
Published by:

      Briggs & Schuster
      BSA.IM

Printed in the United States of America

To my spiritual teacher Eckhart Tolle
for shining the light on the path to the
unknowable, the infinite the eternal

Down to my knees in humility and eternal gratitude to Eckhart Tolle and his teachings. A special thanks to Oprah Winfrey for introducing me to Eckhart Tolle through her TV show Super Soul Sunday on the Oprah Winfrey Network. Absolutely grateful to Esther Hicks for mentioning Jane Roberts in one of her videos and to the late Jane Roberts for channeling this inspirational book The Nature of Personal Reality, a book by Seth. To my son who taught me unconditional love a key attribute of the Unknowable. There are days that I can experience the Presence of SETH as I continue to write this book.

Preface

The author has chosen the title "Journey Towards the Unknowable – The Infinite and the Eternal" from the profound discernment of absolute truth that years of pain and suffering can become our greatest spiritual teacher and all the *Sadhana* (spiritual practice) leads a spiritual seeker to understand that what is absolute is the state of unknowingness—to dwell in the state of unknowingness is blissful that is the space of true wisdom, pure intelligence.

What prevents us from experiencing this bliss is a conditioned pattern that has existed in the human mind for thousands of years to create its own pseudo reality through **limiting beliefs**. That is probably why in the Hindu Vedantic tradition the word *Maya* (illusion) is used for the world we create. I heard my mother reference *Maya* all throughout my childhood but never understood its true meaning until now. This illusory world is created by all humans through identification with a world view(s) not experiencing reality for what it is with crystal clarity but viewing reality through the filters created as energy formations of thought forms, mental constructs we shall label as "limiting beliefs." These limit our infinite potential, the infinite expansion of consciousness of who we truly are in our essence.

My encounter with limiting beliefs was quite an incredibly amazing synchronistic experience. I wanted to share this to show how life unfolds with ease when we are acknowledging the interconnectedness of life and appreciating the synchronicities that unfold no matter how insignificant when we are in alignment with our Inner Beingness—some call it Grace—where miracles arise. The Grace that is this body of work in the form of this book is the result of the unfolding of such a series of miracles/synchronicities.

In the first half 2019, I subscribed to the coursework offered by Eckhart Tolle's School of Awakening. The course curriculum was designed for six months (January through June), so I made the conscious decision to focus and dedicate those months completely to the lessons and teachings—it seemed like I was constantly just watching, listening and reading Tolle content. (I had also cancelled my cable subscription for the past several years to control the bombardment of information flowing into my Being.) One day, as a relief from this hypnotic trance of Tolle content, I had to resort to my only recourse which was to look for content on Amazon Prime or YouTube. I pulled up the Amazon Prime list and in a strange coincidence saw a course that my son had subscribed to on Gnosticism by Professor David Brakke (a part of "The Great Courses.") I have always been interested in understanding the mystical traditions of other religions and an intuitive understanding that all traditions/religions are teaching the same fundamental truth. I watched the lessons, and the key point I took away is that Gnostics believe we are all descendants of Seth.

After a month or so of learning about Gnosticism, I looked for additional spiritual content on YouTube—material that was not related to Tolle. Due to YouTube's algorithms, the first video that I was presented with was Abraham Hicks, so I watched a few of her videos on the law of attraction. In one video, she stated that Esther and Jerry Hicks learnt their channeled teachings after meeting Jane Roberts, who channeled this non-physical entity Seth. The moment I heard those words, I had goosebumps—a state of joy that somehow all this is interrelated. Why randomly pick a coursework in Gnosticism which mentions Seth and now Abraham Hicks mentions Seth.

A few months passed by and I was explaining to my son this synchronicity with "Seth" references coming up over and over again. Subsequently, I tapped on the YouTube app on my phone and the first video that appeared was the audio book *Seth Speaks*, written by Jane Roberts through the channeled teachings of Seth—more goosebumps at the synchronicity. Once I discovered that one audiobook, I searched for additional releases to listen to during my long commute. I found the book *The Nature of Personal Reality* (also by Jane Roberts), which was yet another channeled teaching of Seth.

Combining *The Nature of Personal Reality* with Tolle's teachings has made quite a radical transformation in me. I have concluded that the pain and suffering that humans encounter is due to limiting beliefs, including my very own. I have subsequently used these principles of examining limiting beliefs with others around me as well as in posts on Facebook groups that are based on Tolle's teachings, and have managed to create quite a few jaw-dropping, aha moments in these posts and conversations. *The Nature of Personal Reality* also extensively talks about limiting beliefs—feel free to explore this book as well to gain more of an understanding of how these are created. I will mention a few concepts from the book here in combination with Tolle's teachings of the pain body and collective conditioning. Due to the phenomenal feedback from people that I have met and the social media responses, the idea arose to compile all this information into a book—this combination of Tolle's teachings in conjunction with the principles taught in *The Nature of Personal Reality*.

I explain all these events that took place within the span of seven months to show how when one is in alignment with inner Beingness/Presence/Awareness, synchronicity can be that explosive yang energy of creativity acting as a catalyst that provides the impetus and propels us constantly towards our destination, goal and outer purpose to achieve our infinite potential.

Synchronicities are the bursts in the energy field of infinite possibilities that inject a boost of enthusiasm in us—and that enthusiasm is like switch rails on a railroad track shifting us towards our ultimate purpose. I would never have imagined that I would ever write a book, much less this year.

This book goes on to show this yang energy of creativity is available to each human, that we are the ultimate co-creators of our past reality and take responsibility for it as well as our present reality, where we are empowered to live out our infinite potential, bringing about greater abundance in joy, prosperity and health to achieve a peak of well-being in our day-to-day living. Planetary intelligence, the INFINITE/The UNKNOWABLE has endless abundance in store for all of its creations, including humans.

Chapter 1
The Unknowable – The Infinite and the Eternal

This book is an invitation to you to join me on this journey into the unknowable. If you are reading the word "unknowable" in the context of a spiritual teaching for the first time, you may be naturally curious as to what that means. The unknowable is our conscious connection to the unmanifested Source/God/planetary intelligence, Eckhart Tolle often states in our essence we are an invisible formlessness so ultimately unknowable but with infinite depth. So, the journey towards the unknowable is to experience our essential formlessness, invisible essence in every present moment as a continual process. Abraham Hicks uses the term "non-physical energy," that we are created of non-physical energy—the same as Tolle's formlessness and invisible essence—to be ONE with All that IS, where One is All and All is ONE as is stated in one of my meditations by Sacred Acoustics.

Other than humans, all other forms that are created in this Cosmos—from a rudimentary stone, to a single celled organism, to all of the aquatic creatures, to all the creatures that live on land, to minerals, plants, flowers and trees, animate and inanimate forms—seem to understand the hidden harmony of the Cosmos and live in complete alignment with and maintain this conscious connection to the unmanifested. Unlike humans, all these forms rise and fall, living to their fullest potential, wither and decay with ease, life becomes one seamless orchestration of melodious symphony, reaching the crescendo at death.

Chapter one of *The Nature of Personal Reality* states the following about this hidden harmony:

"The living picture of the world grows within the mind. The world it appears to you is like a three-dimensional painting in which each individual takes a hand. Each color, each line that appears within it has first been painted within a mind, and only then does it materialize without.

In this case, however, the artists themselves are a portion of the painting, and appear within it. There is no effect in the exterior world that does not spring from an inner source. There is no motion that does not first occur with the mind. The great creativity of consciousness is your heritage. It does not belong to mankind alone, however. Each living being possesses it, and the living world consists of a spontaneous cooperation that exists between the smallest and the highest, the greatest and the lowly, between the atoms and the molecules and the conscious, reasoning mind.

All manner of insects, birds and beasts cooperate in this venture, producing the natural environment. This is as normal and inevitable as the fact that your breath causes a mist to form on glass if you breathe upon it. All consciousness creates the world, rising out of feeling-tone. It is a natural product of what your consciousness is. Feelings and emotions emerge into reality in certain specific ways. Thoughts appear growing on the bed already laid. The seasons spring up, formed by ancient feeling-tones, having deep and abiding rhythms."

The journey towards the unknowable and the infinite is a journey into living out our true purpose, living as the rest of creation does in this One Verse (Universe), self-aware of our interconnectedness with the Cosmos, the infinite abundance available to all of creation, in constant alignment with Source/planetary intelligence which leads us to live out our infinite potential with pure blissful joy, soaking up each experience into our consciousness on a cellular level in every present moment through laws of resonance, attracting abundance, an overall balance and well-being of body, mind and spirit.

Tolle uses the term "evolutionary impulse of the Universe" in his book *A New Earth* to explain this phenomenon. It is an evolutionary impulse because this formlessness invisible essence, this non-physical energy, wants to expand through this human form to infinity—that is why in "finite words" the indescribable is called the infinite and the eternal (God/planetary intelligence). So, there is a constant push notification from this non-physical energy in the form of challenging experiences that arise (extreme pain and suffering) when we are out of alignment with Source/God and out of alignment with the evolutionary impulse to expand to infinity—the Big Bang. The push notifications in the form of badges, banner notifications and loud beeps/sirens of planetary intelligence alerting us to nonalignment with Source/God come in the form of the feeling tone of emotions, such as discontent, boredom, anger, annoyance, frustration, depression, anxiety driven and fear. When we are in alignment we are living at our highest potential, we are bursting with creativity, innovation, experiencing abundance, humility, gratitude, loving kindness, compassion and empathy.

As a feeling-tone, this vibrational energy of resistance of the identified mind is experienced as a low-lying discontent. If we have enough awareness/Presence/alignment with inner Beingness in us, we can begin to notice this low-lying discontent and boredom, of not being comfortable in our skin, of a sense of lack and incompleteness (terms used by Tolle), which are lower frequency vibrations. The feeling-tone of emotions of love, gratitude, humility, compassion and empathy are of high-vibrational frequency.

Invariably, if we continue to refuse to

participate in this evolutionary impulse, we **co-create** pain and suffering not only for ourselves but through laws of resonance/attraction we also inflict pain and suffering on all of those around us, the family we live with, the city/state/country in which we live and, in turn, on this planet. The primary reason why there is so much chaos and turmoil on this planet, Tolle explains in *The Power on Now*, is *"The pollution of the planet is only an external reflection of an internal psychic pollution: millions of unconscious individuals not taking responsibility for their inner space."* Approximately 7.6 billion individuals not completely aligned with Source/planetary intelligence with the unmanifested spiritually unconscious therefore causing chaos and turmoil. Tolle often states in his talks that in this time and age we experience more and more suffering not through natural calamities but through humans inflicting pain and suffering on each other. (The book you're reading right now is best read in conjunction with Tolle's books *The Power of Now* and *A New Earth* as many of the terms that I use are based on his teachings.)

You may logically then wonder, "What is it that prevents me from being the unknowable, my formlessness, not in alignment with Source/planetary intelligence, cut off from any abundance and joy?" The answer lies in the separation that the mind energy causes in the form of lower frequencies of vibration of negative thoughts and the corresponding feeling tone of emotions that those thoughts feed, the content in Awareness.

Mankind has been doing so for thousands of years so this is a conditioned pattern. Most of these thoughts that are feeding the emotions can be generically labeled as limiting beliefs. Therefore, a lot of what this book will examine is our limiting beliefs, but before we start with that, a primary requirement is the birthing of the transcendent dimension of Presence in order to examine our inner states, observe our mind and the deep-seated limiting beliefs that are lodged in us at the energetic levels that we never knew existed.

Presence/Awareness – Intensifying Presence, Alignment with Inner Beingness

Understanding and dissolving our limiting beliefs requires a non-judgmental examination or observation of our mind, vibrational energy, thoughts, emotions and life situations of the present moment, which can only be performed when this other faculty (Presence) has arisen in us. Tolle calls Presence the transcendent dimension and quotes Jesus as saying, "The Kingdom of Heaven is within us," or referring to Presence as our "Buddha nature" or "Pure awareness." Tolle seems to have used the terms Awareness, Presence and Beingness as interchangeable for the transcendent dimension. As is often attributed to Albert Einstein "problems cannot be solved at the same state of consciousness that created it." So, to solve our so-called problems, the transcendent dimension of Presence needs to arise to help us see with crystal clarity the objects in our Awareness—the content of our thoughts, beliefs and emotions—to examine their intention and impulse of that particular thought and the corresponding emotion that is caused by that thought pattern. In *A New Earth*, Tolle says, *"The seeing is freeing,"* meaning once we direct the attention, we dissolve the pattern. Then, we subsequently dissolve the content of our beliefs and patterns and raise our vibrational frequency which through laws of resonance attracts harmony, well-being and abundance.

If this Presence/Awareness/alignment with inner Beingness is not arising in us then the Ego/identified mind (which is very cunning and clever) will come in and say, "Ah, that's not going to work out." Or if we examine a limiting belief it will come in and say, "Nah, I don't believe that, that is not what is causing my challenges at the present moment, how can that belief cause this challenge?" Abraham Hicks uses the term "wobble"—that there is a wobbling, a flip flopping, when the ego is involved. Or even worse is the spiritual unconsciousness of not even detecting the thought pattern of the belief at all.

This is how the flip flop/wobble of the ego works: Say we are examining the belief, "I don't know how to manage my clutter" then the Ego/identified mind will come in and say, "But clutter is good, it is my individualism," and keep defending why we have so much clutter instead of non-judgmentally observing why we have so much clutter. Observe the mind, how it flip flops: "I have clutter," "No, I am not the creator of my clutter," "No, clutter does not mean that I have a confused mind," and so on. The steadfast Presence/Awareness/alignment with Inner Beingness is needed to shut the mind energy down and examine our thoughts from a non-polarized view, see reality exactly for what it is—pure, plain, naked facts—and see our beliefs for exactly what they are, which is co-creating our reality and challenging life situations.

In *The Power of Now*, Tolle also offers this pointer that can be easily missed: *"So deal with the past on the level of the present. The more attention you give to the past, the more you energize it, and the more likely you are to make a 'self' out of it. Don't misunderstand: Attention is essential, but not to the past as past. Give attention to the present; give attention to your behavior, to your reactions, moods, thoughts, emotions, fears, and desires as they occur in the present. There's the past in you. If you can be present enough to watch all those things, not critically or analytically, but non-judgmentally, then you are dealing with the past and dissolving it through the power of your presence."*

We could go to a psychotherapist and explain our problems, have several sessions and dig deep into our history, but what has been imprinted on us at the energetic level of our non-physical energy as conditioned patterns can only be known through this non-judgmental examination from Presence because no therapist or spiritual teacher is constantly with us throughout the day monitoring our inner state—but Presence is relentlessly there, the eternal within. As Tolle says, the wisdom always arises from within, so no matter how many spiritual teachers we follow or how many therapy sessions we attend, ultimate liberation from our patterns only arises from our own inner wisdom, from this non-conceptual intelligence of Presence, alignment with inner Beingness.

The additional benefit to a good Presence practice and developing Presence power is the amount of natural healing that it brings into our physical body. So not only can we heal the physical, we can also heal the psychological disharmony, if we are experiencing depression, anxiety, increased anger, annoyance, etc., all these dissolve. In general, there is a balancing of psychological and physical health in the human.

Presence Practices

The next logical question is, "How do I develop this Presence power?" Every human has had glimpses of this state of Presence—they've had a transcendent experience like being on a beach and seeing a beautiful sunrise, or meeting with a loved one that we haven't seen for years and we are bursting into a state of joy, or when we looked into the eyes of a dog that looks back at us with unconditional love, or when we fell in love with a partner and saw our love mirrored by the other. There are times that we hold a baby and the baby looks back at us with unconditional love, or we hike up a mountain and sat still in nature—those can all be moments of Presence. Many people experience their Presence when they go to a new place on vacation and enjoy the unique attractions. Some people, a fact that Tolle has brought up in his talks many times, engage in dangerous activities, such as mountain climbing, paragliding, diving, snowboarding/skiing, etc. to find Presence. All these are moments of transcendence, but the human is not aware that they are totally present in the moment or that the state of exhilaration from that activity is actually caused by the Presence that is fully and completely flowing through because we are truly in the moment. In their experience, they just think that it was a happy, feel good event.

The key is to take steps to consciously intensify Presence, intensify this continuity of transcendent present moments. The following tools are generally recommended to intensify Presence. (In *The Power of Now*, Tolle mentions many of these.) All those humans that have not had the fireworks kind of awakening moment like the spiritual thought leaders of today—Eckhart Tolle, Byron Katie, Sadhguru, Marianne Williamson, Esther Hicks, etc.—need these tools to start to develop their Presence power. This is exactly what a mindfulness/spiritual retreat, such as going to an ashram in India and studying with a Guru, or spending time in a Buddhist monastery offers, but if we don't have the means to attend a spiritual retreat, we can start these practices on our own.

- Breathwork
- Inner Body meditation
- Meditation
- Communing with nature
- Music

The recommendation is to use the various methods available to us in the 21st century to implement our very own Presence practice like a daily self-hosted retreat. We could pay hundreds of dollars to join an organized event hosted by any spiritual thought leader but if we did not have the means then self-impose a retreat which works equally well. This is what I had to do, use limited funds to purchase a membership to Tolle's website content or meditation sound recordings and impose a daily routine of two hours of meditation, or a combination of breathwork and meditation.

My first glimpse of Presence power wherein I was self-aware of being aware arose from watching Tolle speak during a 2011 talk. Experiencing this, even just through my television, brought me into Presence for a few minutes. Then the curiosity grew to experience more of this vibrational high. The experience of Presence is like a buzz as we begin to feel the life force we are in our Being. Kim Eng mentions it as Chi or Prana—we begin to experience this life force more fully and completely.

There are other methods of meditation, such as Hatha Yoga, Vipassana or Kundalini yoga, that also offer body work and inner body meditation and are great ways to increase our

Presence power.

Kim Eng offers Presence through movement work that allows us this experience of inhabiting our body. She has a Qi-Flow download available on Tolle's website (Yin Yoga) and continues to offer Presence through movement through her website. We may view this with nonchalance— How does just standing in certain poses and moving our hands a certain way help me? Just try it out for a few weeks and see for yourself. In the coursework of School of Awakening Qi-Flow Yoga, practice is recommended at least two times a week.

I have used a combination of Kim Eng's Presence through movement, breathwork and meditation of binaural sound from Sacred Acoustics (https://www.sacredacoustics.com/) to self-impose an hour or two of meditation and the vibrational frequency just rises automatically—we can feel this alignment with our inner Beingness.

The yogic system also recommends high-pranic foods that support the experience of our life force to a higher intensity. Feel free to use diet as a tool for a brief period to see how you feel.

The goal should be that we are experiencing this Presence constantly throughout the day resting in our Presence power as we continue to do our work or chores.

As a general guidance, a daily regimen would constitute the following

1. Day 1
    a. 20 minutes of breathwork
    b. 20 minutes of inner body meditation
    c. 40 minutes of meditation
2. Day 2
    a. 20 minutes of breathwork
    b. 60 minutes of meditation
3. Day 3
    a. 20 minutes of breathwork
    b. 40 minutes of inner body meditation/Presence through movement
4. Day 4
    a. Repeat Day 1
5. Day 5
    a. Repeat Day 2
6. Day 6
    a. Repeat Day 3
7. Day 7
    a. 60 minutes of meditation

There are additional videos that we offer as part of our Youtube channel as well for spiritual work. Please feel free to use these videos.

https://www.youtube.com/channel/
UChUnY-JlmtLM_rdtQQJ-SpQ

Now that you have developed enough Presence power, let's move onto the next step, which is understanding limiting beliefs and subsequently how we co-create our pain and suffering through these beliefs—the ultimate liberation being to dissolve the limiting beliefs.

It may be now that you have a strong Presence practice that the **Invincibility** of Presence/Awareness/alignment with inner Beingness, the Conscious Mind is so evident that you may not want to read further, I would humbly ask to keep going.

Chapter 2
Limiting Beliefs

Co-Creating our life situation in the Present moment

Eckhart Tolle starts Module One of the "Conscious Manifestation" course with, "There is a correspondence between your state of consciousness, and the thoughts in your mind and your circumstances, external circumstances and also that you can influence or change your external circumstance by changing your thoughts, your thinking." In the book *The Nature of Personal Reality*, Seth states, *"You are in physical existence to learn and understand that your energy, translated into feelings, thoughts and emotions, causes all experience. There are no exceptions."* In the same manner, Esther Hicks, who channels the non-physical entity Abraham in her videos on the Law of Attraction, commonly uses the phrase "thoughts become things." One concludes that the common thread running through all Conscious Manifestation/ Law of Attraction teachings is that we are the co-creators of our life experiences. It is a relief to know that we are the co-creators of our experiences of the present moment, that we are self-empowered to modify this experience if it is not joy filled, bringing us abundance and well-being.

The pointer on intensifying Presence was offered in the first chapter of this very book to gently assist the reader to be in a receptive state of consciousness to receive the knowing that we are responsible for co-creating the life situations of our present moment and this self-realization requires a high degree of Presence/ Awareness/alignment with Inner Beingness. The ego, our identified mind energy, will always want to come in and state, "What do you mean I CO-CREATE?!" and will always want to blame something external, a favorite strategy of the ego to enhance its identity (see Tolle's *The Power of Now* and *A New Earth* for explanations on the ego and the identifications that arise). But deep down if we go into the feeling with the empowering thought, "I co-create my reality in the present moment," we will have complete receptivity.

Limiting Beliefs

"You form the fabric of your experience through your own beliefs and expectations. These personal ideas about yourself and the nature of reality will affect your thoughts and emotions. You take your beliefs about reality as truth, and often do not question them. They seem self-explanatory. They appear in your mind as statements of fact, far too obvious for examination. Therefore, they are accepted without question too often. They are not recognized as beliefs about reality but

are instead considered characteristics of reality itself. Frequently such ideas appear, indisputable, so a part of you that it does not occur to you to speculate about their validity. They become invisible assumptions, but they nevertheless color and form your personal experience. Some people, for example, do not question their religious beliefs but accept them as fact. Others find it comparatively easy to recognize such inner assumptions when they appear in a religious context but are quite blind to them in other areas. It is far simpler to recognize your own beliefs in regard to religion, politics or similar subjects, than it is to pinpoint your deepest beliefs about yourself and who and what you are particularly in relationship with your own life. Many individuals are completely blind to their own beliefs about themselves, and the nature of reality. Your own conscious thoughts will give you excellent clues. Often you will find yourself refusing to accept certain thoughts that come to your mind because they conflict with other usually accepted ideas. Your conscious mind is always trying to give you a clear picture, but you often allow preconceived ideas to block out this intelligence." - **The Nature of Personal Reality** (Chapter Two)

This "conscious mind" is what is Presence/ Awareness/alignment with inner Beingness. *The Nature of Personal Reality* is amazing, written in 1973-1974, that talks about Presence power. All that is simply required of any human, irrespective of their background, is to develop their Conscious mind/their Presence/the Awareness/their alignment with inner Beingness; then to use that Conscious Mind—their Presence power, their alignment with inner Beingness—to examine the experiences of their present life situations and relate them to a belief that they hold in memory. The belief being the co-creator of the challenging life situation.

So, a limiting belief is a thought or emotional formation that can be in the form of memories stored in our physical, mental, psychic energy pattern that is blocking the free flow of Presence/Awareness/Conscious Mind/ Beingness.

The term "limiting" is used here because these are the type of thought/emotional energy patterns that cause us to limit the expansion of the non-physical energy that we are in our essence which wants to expand in its creativity, innovation, imagination and intuition to infinity. These limiting beliefs left alone, if not examined, could potentially also cause blockages in the physical form or mental body causing physical and psychological disharmony of the human.

During the Conscious Manifestation course, Tolle has used the following limiting belief as an example that he held as a child; this thought pattern was due to a dysfunctional home life—"Why do bad things always happen to you?" and, of course, he says bad things always happened to him until he came across a book that explained the relationship between thoughts, energy forms and our experiences. Some additional thoughts can be, "I can never be happy," "I am overweight," "My mother/father does not love me," "I am always right, others are always wrong" and so on and so forth.

The Nature of Personal Reality lists quite a few commonly held beliefs that we will examine further in the next chapter along with some that I have encountered through my own life experiences.

Selective Perception – Past Conditioning – Patterns

The most enlightening pointer that I have found through Tolle's teachings was on "selective perception," which is actually the foundational principle, a primary requirement, to understand Law of Attraction/Conscious Manifestation, how we are co-creating our experience repeatedly. Most followers of Tolle don't even realize that throughout his teachings, video lessons and books he has offered pointers related to the Law of Attraction. He has most extensively spoken on this topic in a few of his talks that are published on his website (https://www.eckharttollenow.com/), titled "The Source of all Trust," "Socrates' Greatest Lesson" and "Transcendence through Stillness." There's also a brief mention in his book *The Power of Now*.

I saw how much it applied to me in my present life experiences to the extent that I have chosen it to be the first topic to discuss as far as limiting beliefs are concerned to catch your attention early on. One of the more insidious sides to holding onto a "mental construct" or a limiting belief is how our perceptions become selective, so we end up repeatedly co-creating the same type of challenging events. In the preface of *The Nature of Personal Reality*, Seth states, *"Experience is the product of the mind, the spirit, conscious thoughts and feelings and unconscious thoughts and feelings. These together form the reality that you know. You are hardly at the mercy of a reality, therefore that exists apart from yourself, or is thrust upon you. You are so intimately connected with the physical events composing your life experience that often you cannot distinguish between the seemingly material occurrences and the thoughts, expectations, and desires that gave them birth. If they are strongly negative characteristics present in your most intimate thoughts, if these actually form bars between you and a more full life, still you often look through the bars, not seeing them. Until they are recognized they are impediments. Even obstacles have a reason for being. If they are your own, then it is up to you to recognize them and discover the circumstances behind their existence."*

This is what is termed "**selective perception**," the co-creator of the similar type of challenges, "the strongly negative characteristics" of our thoughts creating our so-called negative experiences, a repetitive cycle in which we are **imprisoned** in our own selective perception. This is what the Buddhist reference to as the Wheel of Karma, or the cyclical experiences that we co-create from our selective perception—the reincarnation from one thought form into another and the similar thoughts creating experiences in our present moment that are similar in nature and we don't see a way out. It is like when we think of a red car while driving—once we think about that, all we see are red cars. This is an amazing self-realization that all humans are re-cycling experiences. Look back into your life and see how all humans around you—relatives, families, co-workers and friends—experience the same life situations repeatedly (and we consider this "normal" living?).

Tolle has used similar terms paraphrasing here in his 2012 talk on Socrates, that our judgements become a prison—not only do we have the other person held in that judgment, we ourselves are held in that prison. Tolle says in *A New Earth* that if the shutters are closed, the sunlight cannot come in. Then our perceptions become selective. If we call someone a liar who betrayed us, then **we don't even see all the times that this person did not lie**. If we have the perception that our father/mother did not love us, we miss all the opportunities that they did show us love—that is how **narrow-minded** our perceptions and expectations become. Then the other rises to meet that expectation and the flaw amplifies another pointer that Eckhart Tolle makes in his talk "You are the Sky." We do not realize that the amplification of the flaw is in our judgment, not the other person. It is like telling oneself, "My relative/son/daughter is addicted to drugs," not realizing that the addiction is amplified because we are holding onto the belief and all we see is the addiction in our child/relative instead of seeing them as humans with infinite potential.

Along with our selective perceptions, another co-creator of our present experience is what is called "conditioned patterns of the past." Tolle uses the term "past conditioned patterns" or "dense karmic accumulations" to explain the patterns of reactivity that are ingrained in human beings. These are predispositions, the human being may be born in a certain violent or peaceful environment, the "pain-body" being part of these patterns. In his talk "Inviting Presence" Tolle states (paraphrased), "Only when the Presence power grows in you, can we deal with the Eastern karmic stuff. Those accumulations in you that are old patterns, some of which are originating from the present lifetime or childhood, or in many cases patterns going back a long time, how your ancestors acted out these patterns, how your ancestors acted 500 years ago, 1,000 years ago or 2000 years ago, or if you look in terms of genetics or in terms of past lifetimes.

The fact is there are accumulations in you; patterns of unconsciousness (spiritually) that you have had for a long time—karmic meaning unconscious patterns that you identify with as yourself they take you over completely. The truth is real karma is not the external events in your life; the external events in your life trigger the karma that you carry inside, they turn into your reactions and your reactions in turn create what happens to you in your life."

Different people react to the same event in a different manner at the vibrational level. Consider something as simple as the weather: one person may accept the weather as it is, whereas another could complain about it all day. Therefore, we find ourselves in this world with certain unconscious (spiritually) past conditioning that is part of karma that runs our lives and we are totally unaware of it. This is best explained through video: https://youtu.be/Pr5Nfh_D_zY.

When there is no Awareness/Presence in us we tend to repeat the same spiritually unconscious patterns of the past and consider it normal. For example, in my case, I had a strong resentment for my mother's verbal and physical abuse and held onto that resentment (a past-conditioned pattern of humans in the collective consciousness is to hold onto resentments and grievances). Once we have that resentment, then we have relationships with people that are verbally and physically abusive and then co-create, partners that are abusive, children that are abusive, other relatives that are abusive, co-workers that could be verbally and physically abusive, managers that are abusive or work for companies that are somehow taking advantage of us and being abusive, etc. We could be taken advantage of in everyday life when we are overcharged for groceries, or a car mechanic overcharges us for repairs that are not needed on the car or when we go to the doctor and are prescribed all kinds of medication and therapies that are not needed. All we end up experiencing is abuse until we recognize the pattern from Awareness/Presence and dissolve it.

In one of his YouTube videos Sadhguru explains the meaning of enlightenment paraphrasing here as something that he discovered when painting a wall with color.

Trying to make the task easier, he dipped the brush into the paint and then went from one end of the wall to the other with the brush—when he really looked at the results, he realized this is self-realization: we go from the thick paint on one side of the wall where the paint brush was dipped into the paint to being so very translucent as consciousness grows where the paint fades to the extremely faintest of colors.

   If we apply the same analogy to the dense karmic accumulation, the memories that are written into our energy states, we discover that consciousness is subtle, formless, invisible energy. What most humans do is take that formlessness and then add onto it a thicker energy formation in the form of thoughts and make it slightly denser. Thoughts then lead to a feeling-tone of a negative emotion (irritation, annoyance, boredom, anger, depression, anxiety, fear, frustration) etc. For example, if this thought form grows into a strong mental position such as "I hate all men" along with the opinion goes this feeling-tone of discomfort of hate and anger towards men. So instead of living out our true inner purpose becoming more and more transparent—formless, invisible energy formation by allowing more and more pure consciousness to come through this physical form (the faintest color of the paint brush stroke)—we are moving in the reverse direction of the paint brush (the thick paint the first brush stroke) by adding more and more solidity and structure to the karmic accumulation while keeping it alive as thought forms/strong mental positions along with emotions, that arise as the content in our awareness as Tolle says.

That is why Jiddu Krishnamurti calls awareness "choiceless awareness" or "thoughtless awareness" where there are no thoughts, when we are in the state of no thought, we are truly our pure consciousness, an empty state, our infinite state of potentiation. As Abraham Hicks states in one of her lessons, thoughts and more thoughts gather momentum and lead to a belief and more and beliefs lead to strong opinions and grievances, paraphrasing here. So, from the faint paint to the thicker paint of a freshly dipped brush that has gathered paint/content, in the case of the human mind this gathered karmic memory/content is converted to thoughts by words and language. A grievance or resentment 20-30 years later may still have been held in this slightly more solid energy form, thought forms. As these thicker thought forms stay in our field of awareness then through law of attraction/consciousness manifestation, they manifest a life situation that is challenging. More solidity is added to this strong mental position. Now the slightly solidified waveform is gathering more structure and changing into a particle and, soon enough, into matter. The challenging life situation thus now has manifested pain and suffering into our lives through material loss, loss of a loved one, loss of a job, loss of a relationship, through loss of health in an illness, loss of finances, etc. That is why there are so many New Age teachings of mind over matter, the "conscious mind." Therefore, by that token the goal, or our inner purpose, is to move from the slightly solid thought forms to the subtlest of formlessness, invisible essence—from the thicker paint stroke to the faintest.

In *A New Earth* and during the Conscious Manifestation course, Tolle has used the example of humans that have a fear around money due to financial problems as a child.

"For example, if a child grows up with parents for whom financial issues are the source of frequent drama and conflict, he or she may absorb the parents' fear around money and develop a pain-body that is triggered whenever financial issues are involved. The child as an adult gets upset or angry even over insignificant amounts of money. Behind the upset or anger lies issues of survival and intense fear. I have seen spiritual, that is to say, relatively conscious, people who started to shout, blame, and make accusations the moment they picked up the phone to talk to their stockbroker or realtor. Just as there is a health warning on every package of cigarettes, perhaps there should be similar warnings on every banknote and bank statement: Money can activate the pain-body and cause complete unconsciousness.

Someone who in childhood was neglected or abandoned by one or both parents will likely develop a pain-body that becomes triggered in any situation that resonates even remotely with their primordial pain of abandonment. A friend arriving a few minutes late to pick them up at the airport or a spouse coming home late can trigger a major pain-body attack. If their partner or spouse leaves them or dies, the emotional pain they experience goes far beyond the pain that is natural in such a situation. It may be intense anguish, long-lasting, incapacitating depression, or obsessive anger." From *"A New Earth."*

A clearer illustration of what these dense karmic accumulations are can be gained through the teachings from Sadhguru, derived from the Yogic sciences, that everything in our life is run by memory and there are imprints on our physical body, mental body and pranic body. Here is a link to the video explaining this https://youtu.be/qMryd4gurQk. This memory is called Karma, or the dense karmic accumulation that Tolle talks about. Without the transcendent dimension of Presence/Awareness/inner alignment with Inner Beingness the Conscious Mind, we tend to perform actions like a robot just repeating the conditioned patterns of the past, with reactivity due to the memories stored at the energetic level in the human mechanism.

These compulsions and tendencies become our past conditioning, behavioral patterns that we all continue to act upon. All that is required to achieve liberation is to drop these patterns, recognize our compulsions and tendencies that is true FREE WILL. The FREE WILL to co-create a radically different present moment experience.

Some of these collective patterns that we will examine in our limiting beliefs, arise from the country we were born in, the culture we were born in, the family we belong to, the generational patterns that exist in our family, the people that we are around, the environment that we are in, etc.

The Rapid Growth of Negative thoughts

Another key pointer that I picked up from Jane Roberts' *The Nature of Personal Reality* is that thoughts have an invisible light, an inaudible sound and electromagnetic frequency to them. From page 83 of chapter 5:

"As I mentioned earlier, your thoughts have a very definite vital reality. Beliefs are thoughts reinforced by imagination and emotion concerning the nature of your reality.

Now thoughts in general possess an electromagnetic reality, but whether you know it or not, they also have an inner sound value. You know the importance of exterior sound. It is used as a method of communication, but it is a by-product of many other events and it affects the physical atmosphere. Now the same is true about what I will call inner sound, the sound of your thoughts within your own head. I am not speaking here of body noises, though you are usually oblivious to these also."

Continuing,"It does not matter in which language you are addressing yourself, for example. The sound is formed by your intent, and the same intent—I am putting this simply now— will have the same sound effect upon the body regardless of the words used."

In another section of the same chapter there is an additional explanation on how then this internal sound with electromagnetic properties becomes a mental image, is incipient matter and therefore causes the materialization of that matter. Here is an excerpt to explain this materialization of our thoughts into matter:

"Now: When you create a mental image in your mind it is composed of the same properties just mentioned. A mental image then is also a pattern of internal sound with electromagnetic properties imbued with certain light values. In a sense, and a very real one, the mental image is incipient matter; and any structure so composed, combining the electromagnetic sound and light values, will automatically try to reproduce itself in physical existence, or materialization. (Long pause.) There is a definite connection, then, with the nature of such images and the way in which your body itself is composed.

(Pause at 9:25.) Electrons, atoms, and molecules* all have their independent interior sound and light values. There are definite sounds produced when messages leap from your nerve ends.** It is very difficult to explain some of this, but there is 'invisible' light, then, and inaudible sound, that affects your body and helps form the pattern about which it constantly emerges."

Therefore, due to the electromagnetic frequency thoughts of the same nature as in negative thoughts attach to other negative thoughts, they have a magnetic pull to them just like electrons, protons and neutrons due to their attraction form an atom and then the atoms form molecules. Just like a cancer cell, negative thoughts rapidly grow and multiply and in the 21st Century, due to negativity dominating the collective consciousness, the magnetic pull of the negative thought patterns of the collective consciousness is rapacious and therefore negative thoughts prevail in our mind. Observe our mind and see how we can experience the joy of a sunset for ten minutes, or the joy of looking at a dog/cat/pet and experiencing its unconditional love or a tasty snack or meal for a half hour and then the rest of the day we are vibrating at the low frequencies of irritation, annoyance, anger sometimes even misery, sadness and depression—these so-called "bad" feeling thoughts multiply and through those feeling tones we experience more and more challenging events.

Additionally, there is one other aspect that contributes to the prolific expansion of negative events in our experience which is the "pain body," a term coined by Tolle in *The Power of Now* and continued to expound on it in *A New Earth*. Here is a quick definition of the pain-body: *"The remnants of pain left behind by every strong negative emotion that is not fully faced, accepted, and then let go of join together to form an energy field that lives in the very cells of your body. It consists not just of childhood pain, but also painful emotions that were added to it later in adolescence and during your adult life, much of it created by the voice of the ego. It is the emotional pain that is your unavoidable companion when a false sense of self is the basis of your life. This energy field of old-but-still-very-much-alive emotion that lives in almost every human being is the pain-body."* (Chapter 5 of *A New Earth* has elaborate details on the pain-body.)

For example, in a 2012 conversation between Steve Taylor and Tolle, paraphrasing Taylor's discussion on the situation of a writer who was quite famous and one day his house burned down and destroyed his current book material. He was going on a run in icy cold weather conditions. He slipped and fell into a stream and broke his spine and almost died. He was taken into the hospital and was paralyzed for more than a year and his wife left him. This example is humbly offered to illustrate the point on how we can multiply our challenges just through some limiting belief or set of conflicting beliefs. Therefore, the probabilities to consciously manifest challenges because of the concentration of negative energy that is the pain body and the dominant negative energy of the collective consciousness in the 21st Century are considerably substantial.

So, one can conclude that our limiting beliefs spiral into negative thoughts due to their electromagnetic properties and adherence and then feed the pain-body and through laws of resonance/attraction and selective perception we just manifest challenges that grow bigger and bigger causing us pain and suffering that just grows exponentially.

Both Tolle and the book *The Nature of Personal Reality* refer to this as thoughts almost being akin to viruses, like a virus has taken over our mind and possesses it.

"You must remember that you dwell always in a natural framework—which means that your thoughts themselves are as natural, say, as the locks of your hair. In what may seem to

you to be an odd analogy I will compare your thoughts with viruses, * for they are alive, always present, responsive, and possess their own kind of mobility. Physically speaking at least, thoughts are chemically propelled, and they travel through the universal body as viruses travel through your temporal form."

So, the only way to alleviate the challenges that are presented to us in our life experiences is to dissolve these limiting beliefs and dissolve our generational and collective patterns. The incentive to delve into our limiting beliefs is to have this deep understanding from Presence that because of the limiting belief and the electromagnetic quality of our thoughts and emotions we are consciously manifesting greater challenges in our life and cutting ourselves off all abundance and well-being. We cut ourselves off because any limiting belief is the product of the identified mind, our personality, our ego which causes a separation from all the components (places, people, things) that would in combination be the overflowing abundance in our life. Esther Hicks (Abraham Hicks) calls it the "cooperative components" as a description for these (places, people, things). That we cut ourselves off from the cooperative components and then manifest lack, shortage, and stress due to the sense of lack and incompleteness a limiting belief within our self, non-conducive circumstances to mental and physical well-being.

So, let's move onto examining these limiting beliefs to dissolve them.

Chapter 3
Overcoming Obstacles and Challenges through dissolving Limiting Beliefs

I am going to dive into an extremely direct process of dissolving the limiting belief—it is a surgical, incisive process so may seem too clinical and unaffected, but it works. There are many members of the Facebook groups, friends and family members that have been offered the same guidance and have come out with flying colors as to their own insights and intuition regarding the challenges of their life situations. The trust that is needed is trust our inner alignment with Inner Beingness—no spiritual teacher or psychotherapy session trumps our own inner guidance mechanism, that is primary; this Presence/Awareness/alignment with inner Beingness is primary and the rock solid foundation for law of attraction and conscious manifestation to be effective.

The first step in examination of our limiting beliefs is to have the clarity of knowing that we are holding onto a limiting belief. If we don't have this recognition and acknowledgement and take responsibility for it through self-awareness, we will not be able to proceed with the cleansing process of dissolving these beliefs, so a certain degree of awareness needs to arise. Until there is a sufficient gap in our thoughts, we are our thoughts and mind energy and so we think the reality that we interpret through our thinking mind is exactly how things should be, not seeing reality for the way it is. Acknowledgment of this helps people let go of interpretations of reality. Since we are one with our thinking mind until awareness arises, we are a bundle of perceptions, expectations, interpretations, beliefs, opinions and know of ourselves as these and defend these as though we were defending our LIFE.

As a second step, the investigation that is required is to first, through Presence/alignment with inner Beingness achieved through our Presence practice, know of our highest vibrational state, use it as a benchmark where we are in a state of exuberant joy—"Sat Chit Ananda," as Tolle states in *A New Earth*. This is the state where we are loving awareness, we are experiencing loving kindness, gratitude, humility, compassion, and empathy. The qualities of pure consciousness of unconditional love, I love the terms that Abraham Hicks uses for this phenomenon. It is like we are on a "high-flying disc", or she says we are "tuned in, tapped in and turned on," completely calibrated with Source.

Even a slight drop in vibrational energy frequency from that state implies that we are in a state of disharmony. We are being presented with a challenging life situation, encountering an obstacle in the flow of Life, that the normal state of ease and the pinnacle state of receptivity is being blocked. If the term "contraction" helps one understand the experience of lowered vibrational frequency, then it is an experience of contraction in our physical and psychic energy field. There are New Age teachings that sometimes reference this as a "contracted state of awareness" as opposed to an "expanded state of awareness" the expanded state being complete alignment with inner Beingness. As they say in *Star Wars*, "there is a disturbance in the force."

A constant vigilance is needed to monitor our inner states, one of the most popular memes from Tolle—*"you attract and manifest whatever corresponds to your inner state"*—is a reference to attention to our inner state, this extreme alertness and vigilance. Relentless monitoring of our inner state is required, because once we detect there is a slight disturbance, we further investigate what is the cause of the disturbance. Is it a person/place that has an energy difference or is there a limiting belief in me that caused the attraction through laws of resonance of this lowered frequency?

This normal drop in vibrational energy may easily escape us and may not even be recognized if we are not using our Presence power to be in a high degree of vigilance, a highly alert state. The slight irritation standing in the grocery store line and waiting is missed. The slight annoyance when someone at work writes an email or speaks on a conference call with a condescending tone is missed. The slight drop in vibrational frequency when a co-worker makes a scathing comment about our appearance or something we said earlier. When someone cuts us off in traffic the surge of frustration is missed.

The low-lying discontent of just going through the motions of life of waking up getting dressed going to work and mechanically going through the motions of eating, drinking and watching television, going to bed and repeating the same pattern day after day, month after month, year after year is missed and we soon get old and death comes knocking on our door and we think we have lived a fulfilled life.

To give an example of the subtlety of this change in vibrational energy I offer an experience from when I changed jobs in September 2019. Prior to 2019 I had been working from home three days a week for a few years due to a change in our work schedule and reporting structure. Then when we were notified of the resource action/right sizing in June, I started working from home completely until September while I was looking for a job. Now my new job required me to come into work five days a week. I noticed that by the end of the day my vibrational energy has changed, and the lowered vibrational energy let me know that I found this change in schedule challenging. Therefore, an event however inconsequential rising in our experience needs to be examined—that is the degree of vigilance that is required. I did not have any kind of irritation, annoyance or anger about it, it was just a lowered frequency from the state of joyful awareness.

As Tolle states ("observe our mind"), it is more so an observation of our vibrational frequency any lowering from the joy of Beingness that is an indicator of non-alignment with Source and the fact that the state needs to be examined—what is the vibrational resistance in the form of a "limiting belief/dense karmic accumulation/past conditioned pattern" that is causing this drop in frequency, irritation, frustration, annoyance, anger, violence, boredom, grief, depression, fear, anxiety?

The third and fourth steps are now that we have detected the lowered vibrational frequency or any negativity (in the form of a slight irritation, annoyance, anger, despair, grief, sadness, anxiety, fear, unease, boredom) as our inner state, we start to look for a pattern in the experience that caused this specific experience. Do I have a limiting belief that became the point of attraction for this experience? Sometimes it is not clear what is the limiting belief—so spin off the question in meditation for an answer to arise as intuition, imagination, or dream state. This is where, on some occasions, a good therapist can detect the pattern in us, since they have encountered so many life situations. *"The seeing is freeing"* I think I have heard Tolle state in *A New Earth*, quite a few times sometimes just seeing that we have a lowered frequency may release the limiting belief.

The fifth step is to apply a life-affirming belief to counter the held limiting belief or just drop it.

The sixth step is to acknowledge that we have healed from the situation; full appreciation of the shift in our inner state as it applies to this limiting belief. The way we know we have healed from the situation is to see how well we are supported in that area of life now that we have shifted our vibrational frequency back to the blissful state, we begin to see free flow of abundance, if our limiting belief was causing issues with physical health then we begin to heal that part of the body. If our limiting belief was lack of finances/poverty, then we begin to see the free flow of abundance in the form of things and funds flowing into our experience.

Process

1. **Acknowledge and recognize that the experience of the present moment arose from a limiting belief.**

2. **Increase our Presence power.**

3. **Examine our present life situation non-judgmentally.**

4. **Map this experience to a belief of a past life situation/experience.**

5. **Drop the belief or replace it with another belief that is life affirming.**

6. **Heal from this situation.**

I will briefly give an example of my aha moment with a limiting belief. I have been overweight for many years and have tried many diet strategies and methods which have failed. After reading *The Nature of Personal Reality*, I was struck by this insight that this may be related to a limiting belief because the book talks about limiting beliefs around being overweight.

Here are the steps as applied to trying to discover this limiting belief of being "overweight."

Step 1 - Acknowledge and recognize that the experience of the present moment arose from a limiting belief: I do completely and fully acknowledge that this weight gain is because of a limiting belief.

Step 2 - Increase our Presence power: I have been meditating for a few years and have experienced higher vibrational states during meditation, so had developed enough Presence power.

Step 3 - Examine our present life situation non-judgmentally: I non-judgmentally examined the life situation of the present moment of being overweight. Sent off the question into the ether during meditation about finding answers to my being overweight.

Step 4 - Map this experience to a belief of a past life situation/experience: I looked for answers in *The Nature of Personal Reality* to map out being overweight with a limiting belief that I might have held in the past. Paraphrasing here one of the limiting beliefs that was stated was if untoward attention was showered upon us when we were children then we tend to gain weight to make ourselves unattractive towards that attention, so I examined this statement and it did not apply to me, since I am 50-something years old and men no longer pay attention to me in that manner. Therefore, I did not see a reason for my current overweight issue.

The second limiting belief in the book was if we have been pushed around then we tend to gain weight to hold our ground, this also does not apply to me. So, the search for answers continued.

I continued my research into what is it that maps to a limiting belief in my past about being overweight when one fine day I ended up opening the book *You Can Heal Your Life*, by Louise L. Hay to look up something for a coworker in another disease state and how it maps to the metaphysical. So, I looked up "overweight" and there was the suggestion that this has to do with security. Brief tangent now to explain the synchronicity that arises when we are truly aligned with Source, that this person asking me the question about their diseased state was actually for me to find an answer to the question I had spun off in meditation about being overweight.

This was the most mind-boggling aha moment for me as I looked back in the past to my experience that has to do with security and know that in 2012 I had experienced a huge financial loss, had to live from paycheck to paycheck for years and a family member had always repeatedly told me that I do not know how to manage finances. So, my weight gain was because of financial instability of the past and somehow this voice in the head telling me that I am not good with my finances stuck with me, buried deep down in my psyche.

Step 5 - Drop the belief or replace it with another belief that is life affirming: To replace this belief now I life affirm every time I am handed over some money, when my paycheck comes in, whenever I can work overtime I life affirm that extra flow of cash. Whenever a bank or financial institution gives me credit or a gift, I acknowledge that free flow of abundance and I affirm that I can create my own abundance. I also acknowledge the fact that since 2012 I have been able to generate funds to support myself and pay my bills and be debt free.

Step 6 - Heal from this situation: I see in myself that the cravings automatically have dropped ever since I came to this self-realization that the cause of my being overweight is related to financial security. I have been able to apply intermittent fasting for more than 16 hours a day and I am looking forward to more changes in my body as time passes.

Additional Scenarios of Limiting Beliefs causing Pain and Suffering

Scenario One

I will bring up the experience of the change in my experience of the job situation all over again wherein after working from home three days a week and then eventually completely working from home June to September of 2019, I took up a job that required me to go into work five days a week. The lowered frequency of depletion of energies was experienced. Applying the six steps here.

Applying the 6 steps

1. Acknowledge and recognize that the experience of the present moment arose from a limiting belief
   a. I knew this was a limiting belief, that I was attached to this resistance in the form of a drop of vibrational frequency.

2. Increase our Presence power
   a. There is already an established meditation routine

3. Examine our present life situation non-judgmentally
   a. I saw the resistance in the form of the lowered energy as resistance to going into work five days a week.

4. Map this experience to a belief of a past life situation/experience
   a. I mapped this to the experience in the past that I had been working from home three out of five days for years and recently I had one hundred percent worked from home rarely going into the office for a few months, mapped it to the limiting belief that "I am entitled to an easy schedule." Our ego always wants to maintain order and the order then was that I could work

from home for a great portion of my work week—so here was the other polarity in the form of chaos of change in schedule due to a new job.

5. Drop the belief, or replace it with another belief that is life affirming
    a. Once I knew this was the reason, I looked at what about the situation was not allowing me to surrender to the life situation, one was traffic and two was going into work. After a week or so of driving into work and learning the traffic patterns I changed my schedule to coming into work early; waking up at 4 a.m. and going into work by 7 a.m., which allowed me to avoid rush hour traffic. This choice of just shifting my schedule was the dissolution of the dropped vibrational energy; the joy of beingness was back in action.
    b. I also started to experience gratitude for the fact that the commute was short (just 7 miles in the opposite direction of rush hour traffic), but, of course, ultimately the gratitude that I had secured another job with such ease and the job was paying my bills

and providing me with food and shelter.

6. We heal from this situation
    a. I now notice that the job that I took is flexible enough that when I want to work from home, I can at will. That the schedule of going into work is not that challenging anymore I meet people and engage with them daily.

Scenario Two

This is another profound insight that I have obtained from listening to the recordings of the teachings of Abraham Hicks, also mentioned in *The Nature of Personal Reality*, (paraphrasing here): for a challenging event to be co-created in our present moment, not only does the limiting belief/thought have to arise in our mind but also arise in the other that is going to inflict the pain and suffering. So, if one says one is going to be met with an accident then not only does that thought of the accident have to arise in us but also arise in the other car driver that is going to hit us. If one says that they have been cheated on about their finances then the person is holding onto a limiting belief of people taking financial advantage of them and the other possessing the greed and exploitation to take another's money without any remorse or sense of repercussions has to also exist so that they can cheat on the person that is holding onto that type of limiting belief. All these spiritually unconscious human beings are our greatest spiritual teachers in the fact that they shine the light on our "limiting belief" and show us the path to enlightenment— freedom from our limiting beliefs so absolutely filled with gratitude for them.

To further illustrate this, I quote the passage in Chapter 15 page 289 of *The Nature of Personal Reality* by Jane Roberts: *"What you must understand is this: Each of the events in each of your lives was 'once' probable. From a given field of action, then, you choose those happenings that will be physically materialized.*

This operates in individual and mass terms. Suppose that today your home was robbed. Yesterday, the theft was one of the innumerable probable events. I chose such an example because more than one person would have to be involved— the victim and the robber. Why was your home ransacked and not your neighbor's home? In one way or another, through your conscious thought you attracted such an event, and drew it from probability into actuality. The occurrence would be an accumulation of energy turned into action and be brought about by corollary beliefs.

You may be convinced that human nature is evil, or that no one is safe from another's aggression, or that people are motivated mainly by greed. Such beliefs attract their own reality. If you have anything worth losing, you are then automatically convinced that someone else will take it from you—or try their hardest to do so. In your own way you send out messages to just such a person. On basic levels your convictions will be quite similar, but one will see himself as a victim and one as the aggressor—that is, each of you will react differently to the same set of beliefs.

However, the two of you are necessary if a crime of that nature is, or is to be, committed."

In discussing this particular insight with a friend who had experienced the unfortunate traumatic experience of a rape, I asked non-judgmentally if she could remember what happened right before this event took place, did she remember having rape as a predominant thought in her mind? She affirmed yes that was the case, she had been watching the news which was dominated by the information of a rapist that was on the prowl in the city for a few hours right before this incident.

To most victims of a traumatic event of this nature this self-realization may seem quite flippant and discouraging because it strips the human of the "victim identity" that had been carrying the story of the violation for many decades, just be compassionate with yourself. On the other hand, if we can use our Presence power to know this truth then it is the most empowering self-awareness, we take our power back from the perpetrator, we come into complete alignment with the realization that we create our reality that the responsibility is all ours and in that recognition let go of our belief.

As we keep dissolving our beliefs, we become the transparent, formlessness, invisible essence, words both Tolle and Kim Eng use for the consciousness flowing through all of creation, what we could call "THE INFINITE/GOD." We live out our Divinity and Godliness.

Scenario two is a person who has experienced a traumatic event in the form of a violation like a rape/molestation. How do they apply the six steps?

Applying the 6 steps

1. Acknowledge and recognize that the experience of the present moment arose from a limiting belief
   a. My friend trusted what I was stating about limiting beliefs and acknowledged that the experiences of the present moment were arising from holding onto a limiting belief.

2. Increase our Presence power
   a. There is already an established meditation routine.

3. Examine our present life situation non-judgmentally
   a. Examine all the current life situations where we are being taken advantage of and violated in the surcharges of the phone company, or the grocery store or the work situation or the government, etc.
   b. That we are being held against our will doing a job that we don't like that we are being taken advantage of in the salary that we are being paid or being taken advantage of

in a workplace situation of sexual harassment.

   c. That our partners or children are taking advantage of us, not giving us the love and appreciation, and taking us for granted so we are being raped in emotional love and support provided by family.

4. Map this experience to a belief of a past life situation/experience

   a. Map this to the limiting belief that "we should not have been violated and raped." Especially if this happened during childhood, the grievance is extremely strong because one limiting belief is compounded with another limiting belief that children should be safeguarded by their elders, parents, relatives; the innocence of a child should never be stolen.

   b. Additionally, acknowledge how we attracted this event into our lives, take responsibility when in Stillness we go back to the 8-year-old child that was looking for approval, love and appreciation from a man and the man/woman misunderstood us and violated us because they were unconscious of their action. In Iyanla Vanzant's book "*Yesterday, I Cried*", the profound truth that

her uncle did not know how to give
her love and in his drunkenness
all he could do was molest her,
paraphrasing this portion, that is a
monumental act of responsibility
how at the metaphysical, psychic
energy level we attracted this
event into our lives. Or there was
something in the news that kept
circulating information about a
rape and through laws of resonance
the dominating frequency in us
at that point in time was a fear of
being raped. Or there were friends
and family members that were
constantly talking about how young
women are raped and to be fearful
and on the lookout for humans in
the form of rapists and sure enough
that dominating frequency led to
our molestation or rape.

5. Drop the belief, or replace it with another
belief that is life affirming
    a. We drop the limiting belief, taking
       full responsibility for the law of
       attraction/conscious manifestation
       that caused this event, that our
       dominant thought formation at that
       point in time was a sense of being a
       victim of a rape or molestation, that
       we were constantly looking over our
       shoulder and with fear and anxiety
       when we met any man/woman

where they may end up taking advantage of us.

b. Acknowledge all the ways in which, despite that event, how many more life situations have arisen in our past where we were well supported, such as being given a ride when we were tired and had a long distance to walk to our destination. Someone offered their home to us for shelter when we had nowhere to go. A friend offered to fund our rent when we were given that eviction notice. These types of events were more numerous than the one event of rape/molestation. But what dominated our mind was this single violation for 20-30 years. I love the words used in *The Nature of Personal Reality*: There was always "Effortless Grace" available to us throughout our life until this present moment.

c. If you are reading this book and resonating with the material then acknowledge all the ways in which the pain and suffering of that event has brought us to this moment where we are on the path to spiritual seeking of knowing who we truly are in our essence, grateful for the Grace in the knowing that the experience has taught us surrender and allowing of what is—acceptance of that past present moment. That all that was is a lesson in forgiveness, forgive the perpetrator for their unconsciousness, and the compassion for the utter powerlessness that had overcome this individual that they had to obtain power by dominating another, physically weaker, human being. That they are powerless in the face of their own past conditioning/karmic accumulation of this compulsion/tendency/greed/exploitation for sex through dominance of another human being.

6. Heal from this situation
   a. Once we have reached that level of compassion and forgiveness we already have healed. We see circumstances arise to support us, now complete strangers are trustworthy and offer protection and safety continually that there is effortless Grace in our life situations and miracles arise abundantly. Acknowledge how in many ways the Universe is always working in our favor as Byron Katie says.

Scenario Three

Our addiction to unhappiness is another limiting belief. As Tolle points out in *The Power of Now*, *"A Course in Miracles rightly points out that, whenever you are unhappy, there is the unconscious belief that the unhappiness 'buys' you what you want. If 'you'—the mind—did not believe that unhappiness works, why would you create it? The fact is, of course, that negativity does not work. Instead of attracting a desirable condition, it stops it from arising. Instead of dissolving an undesirable one, it keeps it in place. It's only 'useful' function is that it strengthens the ego, and that is why the ego loves it."*

I have seen this limiting belief play out in my late mother's life and I know there are many more humans on this planet that are afflicted with the same, the addiction to unhappiness. If we were having a good time as a family, she would create a situation where people got upset and yelled and were devastated and started crying.

This unhappiness in combination with the limiting belief that we are sickly creates complication after complication in our health.

Applying the 6 steps

1. Acknowledge and recognize that the experience of the present moment arose from a limiting belief
   a. Acknowledged that we are holding onto this limiting belief

that unhappiness buys us something.

2. Increase our Presence power
    a. There is an already established meditation routine

3. Examine our life situation non-judgmentally
    a. Recognize that there are many situations in which there is either unhappiness in us or those around us, that we are obsessed with creating drama in our lives; if everything is going well then we have to say something scathing, or be angry at the grocery store clerk, or the attendant at the car wash.
    b. Also, recognize that we are beginning to have disease state in different parts of our body, arthritis of the hand has moved to high blood pressure, moved to hypertension and heart stroke, etc. due to this constant unhappiness, the body is a great reflection of our inner state at the metaphysical level/psychic level.

4. Map this experience to a belief of a past life situation/experience
    a. That in the past our grandmother and great grandmother also had this same conditioned pattern that this

is a generational pattern of the past that we are acting out when there is no self-awareness of being addicted to unhappiness so we drop it. That generationally men/women always displayed a great amount of anger, grief or misery at everyday life situations. If everything was going alright, they had to say one scathing statement to be angry at the help, or the clerk or their grandchild or child, or tell their child what a loser they were in life. The constant bickering and arguments with family members and partners are all this grasping that "unhappiness buys us something."

5. Drop the belief, or replace it with another belief that is life affirming
    a. We begin to grow in our Presence power where giving spaciousness to life situations is predominant. Every time a disturbance arises as frustration or irritation, we notice it and just give that energy vibration of irritation within us spaciousness of Presence so that it dissolves into awareness. The irritation or annoyance then does not snowball into anger or rage.
    b. We start to show appreciation and gratitude for all the ordinary things in our lives, for the water that we

are drinking and the food that we are eating, the fact that we have a warm bed to sleep in, for the fact that we have clean running water to shower and be clean, a job that pays us well enough so that we can pay our bills, etc.

c. We begin to appreciate and be grateful for the peace that passes all understanding that life now flows with ease we can just flow with the life situations as they are.

6. Heal from this situation
   a. We start to bring in healing and wholeness and joy to everyday life.

Scenario Four

In one of his talk's titled "The Mountain and the Valley," Tolle mentions the fact that his mother, paraphrasing here, was very much identified with her looks so when she was 80-something years old, she would look at the declining physical form and would ask, "What should I do?" and "What is there to do?" Tolle says this pattern of wanting to do is very much ingrained in the Western society. My observation would be that this aspect of wanting to keep doing is a universal pattern also existed in my late mother who lived in India was constantly wanting to do something, either wanting to check on the delivery people, check on the maid-servant, constantly check on her grandchildren, etc., she was constantly on the move either doing the dishes, folding laundry, cooking something or cleaning—what Tolle calls low-quality doing because we have not given enough time for Presence to flow into this work. Finally, at the end of the day she would be exhausted and sit and watch some television.

Applying the 6 steps

1. Acknowledge and recognize that the experience of the present moment arose from a limiting belief
   a. Acknowledge that we are holding onto this limiting belief about wanting to fill up our life with some action never in the here and now, always wanting to do the next thing.

2. Increase our Presence power
   a. There is an already established meditation routine, we have increased our depth of Presence to that extent that we can experience how much more we inhabit our inner body.

3. Examine our life situation non-judgmentally
   a. Recognize that there are many situations in which the situation pulls us into doing, we are constantly performing this low-quality doing and the mind wants

to constantly keep us occupied in this thinking or doing with our hands, that we are not in the here and now, but want to be in the next moment, the next thing to do.

4. Map this experience to a belief of a past life situation/experience
    a. In the past our grandmother and great grandmother also had this same conditioned pattern that this is a generational pattern of the past that we are acting out when there is no self-awareness.

5. Drop the belief, or replace it with another belief that is life affirming
    a. We begin to slow down and begin to experience the joy of performing one task at a time, experience the Presence as it flows out of our hands into the doing of the dishes, folding the laundry or writing of the email.

6. Heal from this situation
    a. We are experiencing the joy of imbuing Presence into the task that we are performing always in the here and now, as Tolle says "The joy of Being is the Joy of Being Conscious."

Scenario Five

Parents who in their mind are holding onto a limiting belief that they did not achieve enough success may want to live their lives through deriving a sense of self from their children, so they are constantly pushing their kids to do better in their sports, music, orchestra, piano and have them involved in multiple activities such that the kid really did not get a chance to be a kid.

Applying the 6 steps

1. Acknowledge and recognize that the experience of the present moment arose from a limiting belief
    a. Acknowledge that we are holding onto this limiting belief about wanting to push our children to do better, that their failures of our expectations imply we have failed as a parent. I am not a good parent is the dominating limiting belief.
2. Increase our Presence power
    a. There is an already established meditation routine, we have increased our depth of Presence to that extent that we can experience how much more we inhabit our inner body.
3. Examine our life situation non-judgmentally

a. Recognize that we are identified with the parental role this limiting belief that we are not successful and through the success of our child we are, as Tolle says in *A New Earth* "by act of appropriation" we are as well successful.

4. Map this experience to a belief of a past life situation/experience
    a. That in the past our grandmother and great grandmother also had this same conditioned pattern that this is a generational pattern of the past that our father/mother did the same to us, pushed to achieve better, and experienced physical abuse in the form of spanking if we did not excel at school.

5. Drop the belief, or replace it with another belief that is life affirming
    a. We allow our children to flower into their own unique being, allow them to recognize their own unique talent and experience the success in pursuing that talent whether it was gardening, cooking or writing.

6. Heal from this situation
    a. Our experience and relationships with our child are of unconditional love of a parent that possesses Presence power. It is far healthier and the child is blooming and

growing as a loving, kind, compassionate and empathetic person.

By now the reader should be able to see the challenges of their present moment and map out the challenges into these six steps. There is no present moment experience, thought or emotion that is off limits. They all need to be explored to link these thoughts and emotions (drop in vibrational frequency) back to a limiting belief from the past. We have unlimited access to this knowledge as long as we stay vigilant, keep our conscious mind crystal clear and are in relentless pursuit of curiosity of why we are holding onto this limiting belief, it is the GAME OF LIFE until we take our last breath.

Byron Katie has a similar way of looking at what we are thinking and believing— she uses what is a turnaround to come to the actual mapping of the limiting belief, she says every thought and judgment belongs on paper. She has an incredible talent for uncovering the beliefs as well—please feel free to use her method as well on The Work https://thework.com/.

Abraham Hick/Esther Hicks has a similar teaching because her teachings are based on the Law of Attraction. Please feel free to explore her teachings as well.

Dealing with Obstacles

One common limiting belief is that the arising of obstacles in our lives are "obstacles"— we get discouraged or experience a state of hopelessness, despair, or depression by the life experience in the moment and give up. If we have enough Presence power/alignment with inner beingness we are self-aware that the obstacle is just moving us in another direction, just like a stone in the middle of the river, the curve and downslope is just allowing the water to flow down towards sea level the same way the obstacle is just turning us in the right direction.

For example, in one of my workplace situations inspired after a few years of Presence/Present moment centered living I wanted to share this knowledge with people at work. Couched in the language of business I labeled it "emotional intelligence." So as one of the personal career goals at work I had proposed that I would work towards building and improving the emotional intelligence of the team. I was not quite supported in achieving this goal.

Instead of being discouraged and moving into hopelessness, as Eckhart has elaborated in depth in chapter 10 of *The Power of Now* on the meaning of surrender, I did not take this as an obstacle, I just surrendered to it and moved into a state of acceptance. A few months later there were some changes in our Management structure and our team started reporting to a new senior leader and I was able to work with this leader in presenting Mindfulness as a strategic initiative at the business unit level instead of just at my individual team level.

What seems like an obstacle in our life, something that could be taken as discouragement and what would cause us to give up our vision is just a redirection of our GPS, recalculating our route and repositioning us to the next level of expression of the consciousness flowing through us. If I would have given up once the first obstacle arose, we would not have been able to promote "Mindfulness" as a company wide initiative. It becomes like the stones and boulders in the river or stream that just re-routes the river towards its ultimate destination, the sea and the ocean (Source), the same way the obstacle just re-routes us.

After a few months I was given notice from this company (another route recalculation) as part of their right sizing efforts and had to leave this highly successful endeavor, but my inner knowing that even this is not an obstacle, just Grace, I accepted it. Now in this present moment we use the format of the Mindfulness sessions as a group meditation that is offered to the Facebook community of more than 60 thousand members so that experience of developing a Mindfulness session for our business unit was necessary to prepare the vehicle for the next step, I would never ever have been comfortable in front of a camera if I had not become comfortable with speaking to general managers of my company in front of a camera through the Mindfulness program.

Always implicitly trust this connection to Source, this Presence power that is flowing through us that if our vision is small it will direct us towards expansion of that vision—we are just not able to see the full panoramic magnificent view of this vision in this present moment due to our own limitations. So, a listening mode is constantly required, that is why the daily Presence practice is needed. So the way to dissolve an obstacle is to know that "obstacle" is a label that we are applying to the life situation, the present moment is as it is and how through this vibrational state of allowing/acceptance we consciously manifest a favorable outcome—some label these as miracles.

Deeper Dive into Limiting Beliefs

The commonly listed limiting beliefs in *The Nature of Personal Reality* and some that I have found to be true include the following.

1. "Life is a valley of sorrows"

2. "The body is inferior. As a vehicle of the soul it is automatically degraded, tinged. You may feel that the flesh is inherently bad or evil, that its appetites are wrong. Christians may find the body deplorable, thinking that the soul descended into it—"descent" automatically meaning the change from a higher or better condition to one that is worse. Followers of Eastern religions often feel it their duty, also, to deny the flesh to rise above it and into a state where nothing is desired ('Emptiness' in Taoism, for instance). Using a different vocabulary, they still believe that Earth experience is not desirable in itself."

3. "I am helpless before circumstances that I cannot control."

4. "I am helpless because my personality and character were formed in infancy, and I am at the mercy of my past."

5. "I am helpless because I am at the mercy of events from past lives in other incarnations, over which I now have no control. I must be punished, or I am punishing myself for unkindness done to others in past lives. I must accept the negative aspects of my life because of my karma."

6. "People are basically bad and out to get me."

7. "I have the truth and no one else has. Or, my group has the truth and no other group has."

8. "I will grow frailer, sicker and lose my power as I grow old."

9. "My existence is dependent upon my experience in flesh. When my body dies my consciousness dies with it."

10. "I am sickly and always have been."

11. "There is something wrong with money. People who have it are greedy and less spiritual than those who are poor. They are unhappy and snobs."

I have used the following very engineering-like strategy which is a tabular format to explain what the limiting belief is and its effects. Provided below is a table of beliefs stated above and some that I have encountered, what the effects of the belief are what is the challenge and obstacle we are co-creating by holding such a belief, and then what is the result when we shine the light of consciousness and dissolve that belief, use our Presence power/Awareness/alignment with inner Beingness and know of a more truer statement.

As stated before, Byron Katie has used a similar approach with her process of The Work (https://thework.com/), wherein she asks for every thought to be written down on paper and then examined. Please feel free to use her method as well.

Limiting belief	Effects of belief	Planetary intelligence perspective	Dissolving the belief
I am a victim of a traumatic event	There are various events that we become a victim of: a partner victimizes us, our children victimize us, our job situation victimizes us, ordinary life situations victimize us.	Planetary intelligence is aware of the perfection in the occurrence of that event. It is loving us as well as the perpetrators of the victimization at that point because both are needed, the perpetrator is serving their purpose in helping us evolve into our true self. Grace kept us safe no matter how traumatic the event.	We no longer have events arise in our life that further victimize us. We are self-aware of the lesson in forgiveness and filled with gratitude for the experience that helped us evolve into our true self.

Limiting belief	Effects of belief	Planetary intelligence perspective	Dissolving the belief
Because I am East Indian or African American, I am not considered as a person that tips well at restaurants.	We walk into the restaurant with a feeling of being judged already. Due to this law of attraction we may experience a wait staff that offers poor service.	Planetary intelligence is readying an excellent eating experience for us.	We walk into the restaurants as a pure crystalline energy of Presence in a state of joy of experiencing a high-quality dinner, enjoy interacting with the waiter, give them our Presence and end up having an excellent meal and joy-filled eating experience.
Life is a valley of sorrows	We constantly manifest situations where we experience pain and suffering, failed relationships. All the service industry around us fails us, etc.	Planetary intelligence has a plethora of joyful experiences ready for us to experience, wherein it can enjoy its own creation through our physical form.	The experience of the present moment is as it is, we accept it. We perform right actions with humility, loving kindness, compassion and gratitude. Life flows with joy and ease.

Limiting belief	Effects of belief	Planetary intelligence perspective	Dissolving the belief
I have the truth and no one else has	We are constantly defending our mental position, getting into arguments and lack any kind of agreement, even verbal combat defending our position. These positions may be attached to our opinion as a spiritual person, or attached to our opinion of the political party that we support, the opinion of race, gender, class, region, etc.	Any thought formation is a separation from alignment with inner beingness; planetary intelligence has no opinions.	We state the facts of what needs to be stated with detachment. If the other accepts it then good and even if they don't accept it, we are not affected or devastated by it, we remain calm in a state of non-reaction.

Limiting belief	Effects of belief	Planetary intelligence perspective	Dissolving the belief
The body is inferior	We are denying ourselves good clothes, shoes, things, food to eat. We are addicted to our unhappiness so deny our body normal pleasures. Feeling guilty every time we bought an expensive outfit, shoes, etc.	We were given this life and physical form; enjoy every present moment of this physical form and the mind.	Every item that we possess, we enjoy just having it with us, whether it is a chair, sofa, desk lamp, plain cup or simple shoes. The joy of honoring and holding every item we possess as sacred, with appreciation and gratitude.
There is something wrong with money	We are manifesting poverty for ourselves living paycheck to paycheck and not being able to balance our bills and constantly struggling to make our credit card payments.	There is infinite abundance of wealth available.	We are manifesting and co-creating value into this world therefore are compensated well for our services, we are overflowing with material abundance.

Limiting belief	Effects of belief	Planetary intelligence perspective	Dissolving the belief
I will grow frailer, sicker and lose my power as I grow old.	We are constantly in fear of dying and also of growing old. Due to the law of attraction, we attract an illness that is fatal or we lose our life when we are young.	Life is meant to be lived out fully and completely.	We live each present moment joyfully and full of zest.
As a person of a race other than Caucasian/White, I am Black, Brown or any other color less than and will be discriminated against and treated as less than others, I will not succeed in my career or be given higher paying positions.	I am experiencing more and more situations where I am discriminated against, at the grocery store, at the dry cleaners— any service industry. The same happens at workplace situations as well others are promoted.	All humans are a field of non-physical, formless energy with infinite potential.	People love seeing us, the person at the dry cleaners or grocery store gives us a big hug when they see us. We are given recognition constantly at work and huge promotions.

Limiting belief	Effects of belief	Planetary intelligence perspective	Dissolving the belief
I am a woman so I will be paid less than a man and not be moved to higher paying positions.	I do not get promoted quickly enough, sometimes I am managed out of my jobs or experience a reduction in force, constant instability as far as gainful employment is concerned.	All humans are a field of non-physical, formless energy with infinite potential.	I experience a great deal of respect for the value that I bring to the company and I am moved into jobs that capitalize on my knowledge and skill set.
Other people are out to get my share of success.	There is increased competition and wanting to show that we are far better than the other in corporations/ workplace. We are constantly putting down our co-workers and when they receive recognition and accolades, we are inwardly jealous and envious.	Planetary intelligence is in the joy of creativity and experiences, it blooms in every success.	We join planetary intelligence in experiencing this joy and are joyful when there are accolades showered upon co-workers. We love all the recognition and success that is bestowed upon them.

Limiting belief	Effects of belief	Planetary intelligence perspective	Dissolving the belief
My mother/father does not love me. (This is also transferrable to siblings, relatives and friends.)	We constantly seek love, approval, and appreciation from loved ones, from friends, co-workers and managers. Belief cuts us off from recognizing the times when we are genuinely loved and appreciated which may not show up exactly in the form that we imagined how love should take.	Planetary intelligence is unconditional love, always pouring down that love on us as Grace.	As we experience our Presence, we begin to realize that the source of love was always within us, it does not come from mother, father, friend, family—if it does then that is a bonus.
My religion holds the only sole truth.	We are intolerant of other religions. Even if the words Jesus, Buddha, Gita are mentioned we feel a strong feeling of opposition and wanting to defend our religion that it is the only one that holds the sole truth.	Planetary intelligence has no religion it just is infinite and eternal spaciousness.	We are the infinite and eternal spaciousness in the alignment with inner Beingness.

Limiting belief	Effects of belief	Planetary intelligence perspective	Dissolving the belief
My political party is the one that stands on a value system— others do not.	We are constantly having discussions on social media defending our political party. In conversations we are having heated discussions.	Planetary intelligence has no political party.	We don't identify with any political party.
Men/women are not to be trusted; they always betray me.	We are constantly in relationships with men/ women where they cheat on us.	Planetary intelligence trusts its creation.	We experience joyful relationships with all of creation.
Women are mean and display catty behaviors.	This could happen either way but since our perception has become selective all we encounter is mean and catty behavior.	Planetary intelligence is loving kindness and compassion.	We experience women displaying loving kindness and compassion.
Men/women of blonde hair blue eyes are more beautiful.	We begin to adore men/ women with blonde hair and blue eyes we consider ourselves less than and inferior if we are not the same color.	Planetary intelligence loves all of its creation equally.	We love all of creation equally.

Limiting belief	Effects of belief	Planetary intelligence perspective	Dissolving the belief
Being fair skinned is superior and dark skinned is inferior.	We tend to treat lighter skinned/ fair skinned people as superior so provide them with better service, friendships and consider dark skinned people as not good looking and ugly so look down upon them, creating a separation.	Planetary intelligence loves all of its creation equally.	We love all of creation equally.

Limiting belief	Effects of belief	Planetary intelligence perspective	Dissolving the belief
Possessing designer clothes, handbags, shoes, a big house, luxury cars, etc., makes me superior and classy.	We tend to spend too much money on designer handbags, on designer clothes, big houses, luxury cars even to the extent of having huge amount of debts on our credit cards due to these expenses.	Planetary intelligence enjoys the creation of form so enjoys the play of all forms, luxury or not equally.	We begin to derive joy from all material things equally, the joy of being is experienced in unremarkable things and if it is a designer item then we enjoy knowing the truth of the temporal form that one day this is going to be here and the next day it may be gone and that we can fully and completely enjoy this creation in this moment.
As a woman/man I have to dress a certain way to gain respect in the business world.	We tend to pay too much attention to our clothes and the way we look, again causing a huge amount of debt in spending on services like hair, grooming and clothes.	Planetary intelligence is neutral.	We are a field of Presence when interacting at work, allowing planetary intelligence to work through us.

Limiting belief	Effects of belief	Planetary intelligence perspective	Dissolving the belief
The world is violent and evil; certain parts of the city and countries are more violent.	We constantly are fearful of the world that there is too much violence in the world. Due to selective perception we also only come across all the news articles that are violent. Also, as we become the point of attraction due to the constant focus on this limiting belief more violent events arise in our experience, our car is the one that is damaged or stolen, we are hit by objects, etc. There are mass shootings and events of this nature that occur in the area around us.	Planetary intelligence is unconditional love.	We are reflecting the core of planetary intelligence emanating love, are loving kindness, empathy and compassion.

Limiting belief	Effects of belief	Planetary intelligence perspective	Dissolving the belief
Possessing knowledge is far superior than others.	We read all the books that are available to us and at every instance are expounding on our literacy and how we have more knowledge than the other.	Planetary intelligence is non conceptual, infinite wisdom.	In our Stillness we are in connection with the non-conceptual infinite wisdom.
Anger is a display of strength and superiority because we feel powerless.	We are fearful because of our powerlessness and use our anger as a weapon and are angry about even the simplest of things like food arriving late at a restaurant or the grocery store line being too long, and are constantly agitated.	Planetary intelligence is unconditional love.	The Power is in our alignment with inner beingness in our constant connection with planetary intelligence we trust that connection.
My city/state/country is superior to the others.	We defend our city/state/country in every discussion on social media and have heated arguments.	Planetary intelligence loves all of its creation.	We understand the equality of all nations, that the boundaries are manmade.

As we review this table we become aware of the kind of limiting beliefs that we may hold and how planetary intelligence sees it, and from Presence/alignment with inner Beingness we begin to see the effects of what would happen if we drop the limiting belief—it dissolves and we clear the vibrational, so-called "negative" low frequency from our vibrational energy.

Chapter 4
Restoration of Peace on this Planet

To restore peace on the planet to bring about equitable distribution of well-being in health, prosperity and joy the infinite abundance of which is available to all of creation; this point in time will be when all humanity is endowed with this all-encompassing knowing of the feeling-tone of alignment and harmony with Cosmic Law. Humans, like the rest of creation, will allow the unconditioned consciousness to flow through their form unobstructed. The blockages/obstructions/contracted state of awareness that is caused by the generational patterns, the collective past conditioned patterns, collective and personal limiting beliefs will have been eradicated. In their alignment with inner Beingness/Awareness/Presence every human will be the epicenter of gratitude, humility, loving kindness, compassion and empathy. This is the arising of the new species that Tolle talks about, a new state of consciousness, Christ Consciousness or Buddha nature.

We gain an understanding of the collective and generational patterns just by examining the prevalent news headlines and non-judgmentally examine what are the collective ideas that are floating in that content: the constant intolerance towards members of the other political parties; making another country or region our enemy (as Tolle states, the ego loves its enemies); the patterns of mass violence and threat of riots; the environmental pollution of the planet and the ignorance of the masses of the damage inflicted upon nature; the news of rape, violence and discrimination against a certain gender, class or race; the collective patterns of limiting beliefs or mental positions that humans as a collective are identified with political beliefs, nationality, race, gender identification, social status, geographic location, family that they were born into, etc.

Tolle has expounded upon the collective patterns in *A New Earth* (chapters 3-5). In chapter 3, he has shown us the collective patterns of the ego, the collective pattern of always wanting our mind to stay occupied with thoughts and emotions, like while we are waiting at the doctor's office and we want to pick up a magazine or a newspaper now it requires an electronic device. The collective pattern of fault finding, complaining, holding onto resentments and grievances. In chapter 4, he expounds on the collective pattern of role playing how a customer who walks into the restaurant wants to be served and respected just because they are paying for the food and the waiter in turn is also serving the customer holding them in higher regard instead of two human beings just interacting at the level of Presence in joying the interaction. In chapter 5 on The Pain Body, he touched upon that because women were persecuted and burnt at the stake in the middle ages, they carry a heavy pain body. The same is the case with someone of Native American origin or African American origin, due to the rape and torture of their race they carry a heavy pain body. A profound pointer that Tolle made in one of his talks is that the hippie movement of the 1960s in America was a generation breaking out of the collective patterns of oppression and subjugation, but then since the identified mind, our ego, takes over in the form of me, the "free person and individualism," there were downsides to that liberation. There was an exponential increase in cases of use and addiction to drugs and promiscuousness in society which led to the current problem of mass incarceration due to drug-related activities.

Generational patterns are patterns of behaviors that exist within the family tree. If the great, great, great grandmother or grandfather was paranoid schizophrenic, then the grandmother, mother and daughter may be. If there was violent explosive anger in the great, great, great grandparent, then the grandmother or grandfather has it and now we have it as well. The same applies to patterns of infidelity, patterns of sexual abuse, verbal abuse, patterns of violence towards children or women, etc. Sometimes there is a social upheaval and then a generation breaks out of the generational pattern, such as with the hippie movement, or a child may break out of their generational pattern and be a more compassionate parent, loving person.

So not only are we under the influence of our own personal limiting beliefs but also the generational and collective patterns and as we examine these and drop them the more our crystalline luminous essence shines through. Given below are a few scenarios of the collective/ generational patterns that are influencing a certain human being and making them spiritually unconscious. What happens when we drop all these collective and generational limiting beliefs that we are most identified with and allow the unconditioned consciousness to flow through known as the awakened state of consciousness, self-aware human being?

Please note that all these profiles are fictional and do not apply to any specific person.

Scenario One: A woman of East Indian origin born in a Hindu Brahmin family, in North India

List of Identifications/Beliefs Collective and Generational Limiting Beliefs influencing this human

1. East Indian (Collective/Nationality)

2. South Asian race (Collective/Race)

3. Gender identification with being a woman (Collective/Gender)

4. Religious identification with being Hindu (Collective/Religion)

5. Caste/class identification with being Brahmin (Collective/Caste)

6. Regional identification with being North India (Collective/Region)

7. Verbal abuse (Generational)

8. Physical abuse, hitting (Generational)

9. Obsessive Compulsive behavior of cleaning (Generational)

10. Upper middle class (Collective/Class)

11. Pattern of holding onto resentments and grievances (Generational)

12. Pattern of being addicted to unhappiness (Generational)

13. Patterns of addiction to a substance (Collective/Generational)

14. Patterns of illness (Generational)

15. Sexual predators (Collective Pattern)

Unfoldment of Life under the Influence of Collective/Generational Limiting Beliefs: Hypothetically speaking, as a woman of East Indian origin, the woman is very shy, does not intermix with men very easily. Those become uncomfortable situations, so she stays at home as a stay-at-home mother and limits herself to her family—there are no bonds developed with other people from the opposite gender or geographic region. She would have endured some form of violation in the form of a molestation due to the predatory patterns present in men in her family or family friends, so adds the guilt, shame and secretive behavior around this violation onto her baggage of limiting beliefs. In the nationality of East Indian and Hindu there is a collective pattern of hating people from Pakistan or Muslims in general. Due to the identification with caste she discriminates against people of lower castes and acts in an abusive manner with her maid servants and people of lowly caste. Identified with her religion she has zero tolerance for humans of other religions. Identified with her region she is not comfortable being in South Indian homes and eating the foods and following the South Indian tradition which will inflict pain and suffering on friends that may be South Indian, there are no human bonds developed with families that are from another region. She is verbally and physically abusive towards her family members and children. She causes a lot of pain and suffering for her family from her obsessive-compulsive behavior of wanting everything spic and span and clean; she has no time to give to them since she is always spending her time cleaning and putting things in an organized orderly fashion. Holding onto grievances and resentments she creates enemies in separating herself from other people, constantly losing friends, not on talking terms with her relatives, even siblings, all of her relationships are dysfunctional. Her addiction to unhappiness leads her to be miserable, every day her pain body is constantly looking for unhappiness to feed on, she is creating more drama by her scathing words and actions. Her addiction to substances leads to habits where she is smoking, drinking alcohol or subject to some other type of addiction. Her addiction to being sickly leads her from one illness to another and now she has a complicated issue as far as her health is concerned.

Unfoldment of Life without Collective/ Generational/Personal Limiting Beliefs: She feels extremely comfortable with humans irrespective of gender, so she does well with finding a job and succeeding in her career. She socializes with people of other religions, caste and class so there is a bond and togetherness, loving kindness and empathy with all. She has loving relationships within her family and friends and is joy filled every moment. She is not experiencing any addictions or compulsions; her health and nutrition are balanced. This human now becomes the epicenter of gratitude, humility, loving kindness and empathy.

Scenario Two: African American woman

List of Identifications/Beliefs Collective and Generational Limiting Beliefs Influencing this Human

1. American (Collective/Nationality)

2. African American and/or mixed-race i.e Native American (Collective/Race)

3. Gender identification with being a woman (Collective/Gender)

4. Religious identification with being Protestant or Catholic (Collective/Religion)

5. Caste/class identification with being Lower, middle or upper class (Collective/Caste)

6. Regional identification with being North American (Collective/Region)

7. Verbal abuse, female dominant family unit/absent or emasculated father figures (matriarchal) (Generational)

8. Physical abuse, hitting, incest, abandonment, criminal family members, poverty (Generational)

Unfoldment of Life under the Influence of Collective/Generational Limiting Beliefs: As Tolle mentions, the collective pain body of the African American people that they have already endured the slavery and oppression of being used as labor so there is a collective pattern of resistance against being subjugated and oppressed. Being of mixed race, she has already endured colorism that is prevalent within the African American race so discriminated against for being either dark-skinned or lighter-skinned. Experienced some form of rape, sexual abuse repeatedly as a child of as young as 6-8 years old. Made wrong choices of men as a result and ended up responsible for a family without a father. Endured verbal, physical abuse as a child so grew up with low self-esteem and endured monumental traumatic events throughout her life.

Unfoldment of Life without Collective/ Generational/Personal Limiting Beliefs: The child grows up with a healthy self-esteem, receives a good education and becomes highly successful in their career and starts to give back to the community and country. This human now becomes the epicenter of gratitude, humility, loving kindness and empathy.

Scenario Three: A Jewish male

List of Identifications/beliefs Collective and Generational limiting beliefs influencing this human

1. American (Collective/Nationality)

2. Jewish (Collective/Race)

3. Gender identification with being a male (Collective/Gender)

4. Religious identification with being Jewish (Collective/Religion)

5. From a wealthy family (Collective/Class)

6. Geographic identification (Collective/Region)

7. Identified with religious traditions (Generational)

Unfoldment of Life under the Influence of Collective/Generational Limiting Beliefs: Being male he looks down upon women, aggressively showing his superiority against women at home and at the workplace. He is identified with his mental position, limiting belief of his race as being Jewish and persecuted by the Germans (during WWII) and Muslims. That limiting belief will create enemies in the form of Palestinians and that is what the war in the Middle East is about—two factions identified with their mental positions of their race and their grievances of their past. He is intolerant and constantly in fear of being attacked by people of Germanic origin or white nationalist philosophies; constantly defending his Jewish beliefs and traditions.

Unfoldment of Life without Collective/Generational/Personal Limiting Beliefs: So, the conscious manifestation here would be to socialize with other families that are of German descent to allow the children and inter-racial marriages to occur between German and Jewish or Jewish and Muslim families, that is when we will have peace on Earth. To see myself in the other and to recognize that there is no other there is just the one consciousness.

Scenario Four: A middle-aged Catholic male of Caucasian race, living in the United States

List of Identifications/Beliefs Collective and Generational Limiting Beliefs Influencing this Human

1. American (Collective/Nationality)

2. Aryan/White (Collective/Race)

3. Gender identification with being a male (Collective/Gender)

4. Religious identification with being Catholic (Collective/Religion)

5. Political identification (Republican/Democrat)

6. Class identification with middle class (Collective/Caste)

7. Regional identification with being from a particular state (Collective/Region)

8. Verbal abuse (Generational)

9. Physical abuse, hitting (Generational)

10. Pattern of holding onto resentments and grievances (Generational)

11. Pattern of being addicted to unhappiness (Generational)

12. Patterns of addiction to a substance (Collective/Generational)

13. Patterns of illness (Generational)

14. Sexual predators (Collective Pattern)

Unfoldment of Life under the Influence of Collective/Generational Limiting Beliefs: Experiences the collective pattern of distrust for immigrants; participates in the collective fear that exists for the citizens of the country of people immigrating from Mexico/Colombia/South America that cross the borders illegally. Identified as a Republican he refuses to believe that there are issues with climate change and the environment. Believes the country has lost its jobs to other countries since manufacturing has moved to countries like China and India. Due to the generational patterns that exist in the family, has experienced verbal and physical abuse and, in a lot of cases, sexual abuse. He is now an angry person, holding onto resentments that manifest as lack and incompleteness in the form of losses, loss of jobs, loss of home, etc. To drown his depression and feeling of powerlessness, he is addicted to alcohol.

Unfoldment of Life without Collective/Generational/Personal Limiting Beliefs: He is a middle-aged male that is aware that this country and the planet is endowed with infinite resources and infinite abundance that is available to all, so he welcomes the immigrants of all walks of life. He makes all efforts to support the environment in his day-to-day life and supports organizations that are working towards balancing the carbon footprint on this planet. He is aware of his power and so creates multiple businesses throughout the country that gainfully employees thousands of employees and helps to bring about abundance.

Therefore, to restore complete peace on Earth and to bring equitable distribution of wealth, health and well-being, all humans will have been restored to their original state of living on this planet as a field of Presence/Consciousness—using their conscious mind to balance themselves to get to a state wherein no more personal limiting beliefs exist, no more generational beliefs exists and no more collective limiting beliefs exists. As Tolle states, "The ego loves its enemies"—so we stop creating enemies out of a race, political affiliation or national identity. We are collectively working towards the good of all of humanity and in turn all of Creation, that is true peace on Earth.

Chapter 5
Free Flow of Abundance through Non-Resistance and Gratitude

The free flow of Abundance is available to us when we are in a state of complete non-resistance, surrendered to what is—that is the unrestricted flow of consciousness through the human form. The highest state of receptivity is the vibrational frequency of allowing, surrender and acceptance that is the common thread among all spiritual teachings if we examine the contemporary literature of Michael Singer's *The Surrender Experiment* or Abraham Hicks talking about "The Art of Allowing" or Tolle talking about "The Meaning of Surrender" in *The Power of Now*.

If we are not operating at this high state of frequency, then we are in a contracted state of awareness and blocking either in the physical body or vibrational energy the free flow of life energy and therefore cutting ourselves off and blocking the flow of energy in the form of abundance of health, wealth and prosperity—that is probably why another term for "money" is *currency*...that it is just a current a flow. As we begin to clear out and permanently delete our personal limiting beliefs, generational limiting beliefs and collective limiting beliefs from our memory, this state of surrender becomes our natural state of Being. In *A New Earth*, Tolle talks about the modalities of awakened doing, which are acceptance, joy and enthusiasm. Joy and enthusiasm are higher states of receptivity than acceptance, when we are experiencing the joy of our alignment with inner Beingness we become unstoppable in our co-creation, we become a force of nature.

Through my financial loss in 2012, I have learnt this lesson to the point that it is seared into the cellular levels of my spirit: when we are brought to our knees, to that degree of humility, the only recourse is surrender. Surrender to what is, at that past present moment even if it meant that I had to stage the house to get it sold to generate funds then gave away my decent furniture to create space. If it meant that the house needed painting and small repairs, then it meant calling the person that was going to come in and complete the repairs. If it meant having to inconvenience myself constantly leaving the house to look for a job while sitting at the library so that people could stop by and view the house, then that's what I did. In this surrender, I found the miracle of Grace in August 2012, the money that was deposited into my bank account from the equity of the house was exactly in the week that I was down to my last $1,000 dollars. That same year, in December as the money of the equity of the house was depleting used to pay credit cards, etc., and I was down to the wire, I found a job. That is the Grace in the surrender to the loss where miracles arise. I am sure the readers have quite a few of their own experiences of a similar nature.

The second most important vibrational state that also invites abundance into our lives and is the perfect partner for the vibrational frequency of acceptance is a state of gratitude and appreciation. There are a couple of excerpts by Tolle on this topic of Gratitude that are awe-inspiring, and I have deep adoration for, and I quote them here.

In *A New Earth*, Tolle writes, *"Acknowledging the good that is already in your life is the foundation for all abundance. The fact is: Whatever you think the world is withholding from you, you are withholding from the world. You are withholding it because deep down you think you are small and that you have nothing to give.*

Try this for a couple of weeks and see how it changes your reality: Whatever you think people are withholding from you—praise, appreciation, assistance, loving care, and so on—give it to them. You don't have it? Just act as if you had it, and it will come. Then, soon after you start giving, you will start receiving. You cannot receive what you don't give. Outflow determines inflow. Whatever you think the world is withholding from you, you already have, but unless you allow it to flow out, you won't even know that you have it. This includes abundance. The law that outflow determines inflow is expressed by Jesus in this powerful image: "Give and it will be given to you. Good measure, pressed down, shaken together, running over, will be put into your lap.""

So, one way to gather momentum in receptivity of abundance in our life other than eradicating all our limiting beliefs is also appreciation of simply unremarkable things.

The second excerpt from *A New Earth*: *"The source of all abundance is not outside you. It is part of who you are. However, start by acknowledging and recognizing abundance without. See the fullness of life all around you. The warmth of the sun on your skin, the display of magnificent flowers outside a florist's shop, biting into a succulent fruit, or getting soaked in an abundance of water falling from the sky. The fullness of life is there at every step. The acknowledgment of that abundance that is all around you awakens the dormant abundance within. Then let it flow out. When you smile at a stranger, there is already a minute outflow of energy. You become a giver. Ask yourself often: 'What can I give here; how can I be of service to this person, this situation?' You don't need to own anything to feel abundant, although if you feel abundant consistently things will almost certainly come to you."*

The most profound statement here is, "You don't need to own anything to feel abundant, although if you feel abundant consistently things will almost certainly come to you." We may be in a situation where we don't have a home, car or much financial wealth, when we wake up, we can be in a state of gratitude for our breath. We are in a state of gratitude for the space that we have been given for shelter even if it is temporary housing or a friend's place or a couch or a park bench. We can hold onto our cup of tea or coffee and experience gratitude that we were given a hot drink. If we have a glass of water, then gratitude for holding onto the glass of water and then drinking it and enjoying every sip of the sweetness of life-giving water. When we step out of our space appreciation and gratitude for the sky, the richness of the depth of blues and greys, the Earth for holding our weight and bearing it so gracefully, for the trees and plants that the city planners have planted so well.

As we move about our day experience from Presence the flow of presence into the other, if we are at a grocery store, appreciation and gratitude for all the farmers and all the factory workers, the transportation industry workers that moved the goods from the farm and factories to the grocery stores to provide nourishment for our bodies. The vibrant vitality of the fruits, vegetables and flowers, the depth of greenness in the green leafy vegetables.

As stated above I experienced a financial loss in 2012, lost my home to generate funds out of the equity of the home since I was running out of money, moved into an apartment and subsequently found a job since I was paying down my debt I did not have any funds available to give to charity. Applying this principle of gratitude and appreciation of all that was around me and knowing the fact that I don't need to own anything to feel appreciation even though materially I did not have much to give; I used my workplace situations to express the depths of humility and gratitude. I would always write emails with humility and gratitude. When co-workers responded with work completed, I would respond back sending them accolades for a job well done, recognizing the quality that they displayed in the moment, saying "thank you so very much for the enormous sense of ownership and accountability, totally incredible, absolutely grateful for the help and support." Acknowledging every conference call, every meeting, every human being that came across. It is like the movie Avatar where the term "I see you" was used as a greeting, I was acknowledging through my inner Beingness "I see and acknowledge you and I am grateful for you."

If I had to eat a frugal meal of steamed rice and plain boiled lentils I would remember Tolle's pointer in his 2012 talk on "Socrates Greatest Lesson," in which he said when living in London in a bedsitter (a single room with a place to sleep and sit with two metal rings for a stove) that all he had was Heinz baked beans and toast. Then he had to share the bathroom and there was a line to go to the loo and all it did was give him constipation to wait in line. Even during those sparse conditions if he just had Heinz baked beans and toast then he felt the aliveness in the beans and toast and surrendered to it. Applying that principle, I would be surrendered to the rice and plain boiled yellow lentils and feel the aliveness in that meal. This experience led me to have a knowledge that no matter how impoverished materially we may be, there are always so many ordinary things for which we can be grateful.

Now, a few years later, I have been able to pay down all my debts, due to the financial loss I have become a minimalist in my day-to-day life so there are not very many material things I own—just enough to support myself, the job that I hold covers all my bills so there is not very much more needed. Looking back to my life eight years back, I realize that the lesson of the financial loss was needed to teach me frugality and offer me this experience to know how to attract abundance through Conscious manifestation/law of attraction. As Newton's third law of motion states, every action has an equal and opposite reaction, the same law of attraction applies to our thinking mind, the more acceptance and gratitude in our Beingness, the more we attract abundance.

Gratitude and appreciation are the invitation for infinite abundance in health and prosperity to flow into our lives the momentum of which starts off with appreciation of simple ordinary things. Gratitude is the fundamental teaching of any religious tradition whether Christian, Islam, Hindu or Buddhist. When we are in a state of gratitude and acceptance of what is of every present moment then we are in a state of effortless Grace.

Chapter 6
Forgiveness

One of the most egregious collective limiting beliefs is holding onto resentments and grievances. The resentment through law of attraction/conscious manifestation ends up co-creating repeated so-called "negative" life situations that inflict pain and suffering on the human being causing not only deterioration of the psychological mind but the physical apparatus of our body as well and, through laws of resonance, inflict pain and suffering on those around us. For generations there are families and friends that stop all communication with their own parents or siblings. They refuse to see their own parents or siblings in person for decades, stop having a relationship with each other leading to loneliness, desolation, and depression. So, Forgiveness is a necessary component to eliminating this limiting belief of holding onto resentments and grievances. Forgiveness of an experience of the moment just passed from present moment to past present moment is more necessary so that we don't end up accumulating these fresh new grievances as limiting beliefs that add onto the pain body and through law of attraction/ conscious manifestation generate more harm and suffering on us.

As Tolle writes in *The Power of Now*, *"Forgiveness is to relinquish your grievance and so to let go of grief. It happens naturally once you realize that your grievance serves no purpose except to strengthen a false sense of self. Forgiveness is to offer no resistance to life—to allow life to live through you. The alternatives are pain and suffering, a greatly restricted flow of life energy, and in many cases physical disease."*

Therefore, from our state of Presence/ alignment with inner Beingness, we have this self-awareness that dropping of all resentments and grievances is necessary. By holding onto the resentment, we are just holding onto a mental position, <u>a thought form</u> that shows us that we are right and the other is wrong, and gain a sense of superiority from the self-righteousness which strengthens the ego, the false self, and thoughts are ephemeral, they will eventually dissolve and we will be shown the futility of holding onto the resentment and grievance, through huge material loss (loss of home, loss of employment, loss of relationships, etc.) or a terminal illness. A dissolution is needed of these thought formations—resentments, grievances, judgments, assumptions and expectations—the more we have the thicker paint on the brush, the more the tendency is to manifest pain that we co-create.

The most inspiring passage on forgiveness is the last page of *The Power of Now*, where Tolle states, *"'Forgiveness' is a term that has been in use for 2,000 years, but most people have a very limited view of what it means. You cannot truly forgive yourself or others as long as you derive your sense of self from the past. Only through accessing the power of the Now, which is your own power, can there be true forgiveness. This renders the past powerless, and you realize deeply that nothing you ever did or that was ever done to you could touch even in the slightest the radiant essence of who you are. The whole concept of forgiveness then becomes unnecessary."*

This passage is a powerful, self-empowering statement because it allows us to reclaim our power from the perpetrators of the abuse or trauma that was inflicted on us. From the depths of Presence/alignment with inner Beingness with loving kindness and compassion, we have the empathy for the fact that all that was acted out on us was the **powerlessness** of a human being they were spiritually unconscious of their actions they were acting out their collective and generational patterns of past conditioning and what was done was done to our "BODY" and "MIND," our radiant essence, this Beingness, was never touched. For that matter the body that was abused if it was physical infliction of trauma as in physical abuse or rape/molestation no longer exists because the cells of the body all die and are replaced within 7-10 years—the 6- or 8-year-old that was abused is not even here, but we have kept the event alive due to the ego strengthening itself in the resentment/grievance.

As Tolle says, "Nobody can act beyond their level of consciousness," therefore they could not have acted otherwise, nor could we have acted otherwise in the past. So, embrace compassion for the other as well as ourselves. The life situation should have unfolded in the manner in which it did because that is "what is" or that is "what was" in the past present moment as Byron Katie says, "When you argue with reality, you lose, but only 100 percent of the time."

Additionally, from the core of the passage quoted above from *The Power of Now*, this knowing arises from Presence that whatever the violation, whether it was verbal abuse, physical abuse, sexual abuse or any other violence, that the event affected only our body and psychological mind, but our radiant essence, this formlessness, invisible Presence was never touched since it is unknowable. This profound self-realization is the **point of power** eventually leading to liberation from our psychological pain and suffering.

When we take this power back, we can see with crystal clarity that the co-creator of our life situation was our point of attraction, we were vibrationally offering that frequency that attracted a perpetrator of that specific type, the responsibility was always ours which is the self-realization of true free-will.

To the mind energy of the identified mind, this realization may not be easily digestible and incredible amounts of resistance patterns will arise—the ego will fight its ego death, loud groans and protests of the identified mind may arise: "How could this be that we were the co-creators of our reality? There is no way as a small child I attracted this horrific event into my life." In "The

School of Awakening" course's "The Teacher called Suffering" module, Tolle talks about how seductive it is for the ego to hold onto its victim identity, this story has been such a part of who we think we are, the mental mind made sense of self, the ego. So, the resistance patterns are valid but from Presence observe our mind, recognize these resistance patterns as patterns that exist as part of our past conditioning that will form into limiting beliefs.

To explain this point of attraction and vibrational frequency that causes the violation to arise, here is an example offered in the book *The Nature of Personal Reality* using the example of a criminal and prison guard that the point of attraction and the vibrational frequency of a prisoner and a prison guard is the same. In Chapter 17, Seth states on criminals and their prison wardens: *"Most criminals, in or out of prison, share a sense of powerlessness and a feeling of resentment because of it. Therefore, they seek to assure themselves that they are indeed powerful through antisocial acts, often of violence. They desire to be strong, then, while believing in a lack of personal strength. They have been conditioned, and furthermore have conditioned themselves, to believe that they must fight for any benefits. Aggression becomes a method of survival. Since they believe so strongly in the power of others, and in their own relative powerlessness, they feel forced into aggressive actions almost as preventative measures against greater violence that will be done against them. They feel isolated and alone, unappreciated, filled with rage which is being constantly expressed— in many cases, though not all—through a steady series of minor social crimes. This applies whether* or not major crimes are committed; so, the simple expression of aggression without understanding does not help.

In the case of criminals and their belief systems, aggression has a positive value. It becomes a condition for survival. Many other characteristics that might mitigate such behavior are minimized and can be seen as dangerous by them.

You isolate the criminal element, therefore, in an environment in which any compensation is refused. The entire framework of a prison—with its bars—is a constant reminder to the convict of his situation and reinforces his original difficulty. Any normal home life is denied him; and along with the overall concentration upon the problem at hand, all other stimuli is purposely held to a minimum. In their ways, the warden and guards subscribe to the same set of beliefs as that held by their prisoners—the idea of force and power is accentuated on both sides, and each believes the other its enemy. The guards are certain that the incarcerated are the dregs of the earth and must be held down at all costs. Both sides accept the concept of human aggression and violence as a method of survival."

There are many more examples provided in this book that are equally relatable and one comes to the conclusion on how each event, whether natural disaster or man made calamity or weather anomaly, was caused by the mass collective unconsciousness, the point of attraction of the humans existing at that point in time.

I do have enormous compassion that this realization of being the point of attraction may require years of therapy sessions with a psychiatrist who holds a spiritual depth and engages in therapies of EMDR and brain entrainment, brain painting, etc., or years of Presence centered practice. But when we do, it is like we are able to soar like an eagle—all the weight of our limiting beliefs is lifted, and we feel almost angelic peace that passes all understanding. As we continue to experience the knowing that our point of attraction and vibrational energy at the specific point in time is what creates our reality, we also come to this self-empowering realization that the perpetrator responded to our point of attraction we were co-creating in our reality in the past and take full responsibility for all the events that arose. Equipped with this knowing that in this present moment we can re-imagine and co-create a different set of reality that is the full participation in Conscious Manifestation/ Law of attraction, that is how we attract the free flow of abundance into our lives—love, joy and peace.

Our ultimate purpose in life is to participate in this evolutionary impulse of the Universe (a term coined by Tolle in *A New Earth*), the expansion that started out with the Big Bang with all of Creation to experience this expansion as an integral part of who we are—we can expand to infinity making the inward journey of experiencing our Presence/Alignment with Inner Beingness.

Or an infinite expansion that is outwardly in external form, enjoying every moment of where we are and what we are doing, in our creativity, imagination, intuition which gives rise to synchronicities that bring about miracles. The Joy of Being flowing into all of creation in our day-to-day life and experiencing the vibrancy and vitality around us. It is as simple as if we are driving to work in joy being with the other cars around us, looking at the colors, looking at the sky, enjoy the landscape that changes every day, enjoy touching the keyboard, writing an email, enjoy hosting a conference call or attending one. Enjoy driving to the grocery store, smile at the people that are around us, look at all the man made creation of items at the grocery store and the lush produce, be a field of Presence as we interact with the cashier and exchange a few niceties with them. If we are taking a trip to another city/country in joy, the engagement with the TSA security agent, the people that are around us, the interaction with the barista as they hand us the coffee and the snacks at the coffee shop at the airport. Enjoy the people on the plane and look at the dog that is stowed away under the seat—send loving awareness to the dog and to the baby that is seated in the back of the plane. To the toddler that ran away from its parents and is now looking at us interestingly, give the toddler an object from our handbag to play and experience the flow of Presence into the other. This is the Divine Game "Leela/Lila" as the Hindu Vedantic tradition states, the play of forms as Tolle quotes in *The Power of Now*. Through our physical form, we allow consciousness to play and enjoy its creation and that is infinite expansion into external form.

As we continue this state of acceptance and allowing as discussed in chapter 5, in gratitude and appreciation, we dwell in our Presence/

Awareness/alignment with Inner Beingness, our conscious connection to Source. This Presence which is in its essence formlessness and invisible as Tolle states that which is ultimately "UNKNOWABLE"; the term that Byron Katie has coined the "don't know mind" in that state of consciousness the unfathomable depths of humility is experienced. As we humans continue to dissolve our limiting beliefs and flower into our crystalline luminous stardust being, we begin to self-realize all there is this journey towards the Unknowable this invisible, formlessness devoid of all limiting beliefs, absent any memories at the physical, mental or energy body level.

Along with indescribable joy, honoring and holding sacred every reader of this book, I am in the state of eternal humility and gratitude to the reader for joining me and being my companion on this Journey Towards the Unknowable – THE INFINITE and THE ETERNAL.

A Note From The Publisher

Briggs & Schuster Agency and its publishing division is devoted to publishing books from all genres. We believe that an author's imagination and writing style is the gateway to communicating their vision.

Journey Towards The Unknowable: The Infinite and the Eternal book is voiced exclusively through the author's writing.

What We Believe

We believe that if you are seeking a Journey Towards The Unknowable: The Infinite and the Eternal, you must start by surrendering your life and opinions to the Savior of the world - Yeshua HaMashiach. We believe the Bible presents the only Truth for an abundant Life and connection with our Creator. So, your journey starts when you know The Way.

> *Yeshua said, "I AM the Way — and the Truth and the Life; no one comes to the Father except through me."*
> **John 14:6**

In this book, other ways and systems are presented with words and terms that identify with the author's belief system. These are not the ideologies or beliefs of the publisher. But, in some instances, we identified ideas borrowed from the Bible - The Unknown, Infinite and Eternal. The Holy Scriptures address that in many places, but the Apostle Paul said it well on Acts 17.

> *For as I was walking around, looking at your shrines, I even found an altar which had been inscribed, 'To An Unknown God.' So, the one whom you are already worshipping in ignorance — this is the one I proclaim to you.*
> **Acts 17:23**

We at Briggs & Schuster congratulate you for choosing to read this book. We appreciate the author allowing us to add this publisher's note in her book. We believe the Holy Scriptures are the only true source to guide your journey.